A HEART LOST IN WONDER

LIBRARY OF RELIGIOUS BIOGRAPHY

Mark A. Noll, Kathryn Gin Lum, and Heath W. Carter, series editors

Long overlooked by historians, religion has emerged in recent years as a key factor in understanding the past. From politics to popular culture, from social struggles to the rhythms of family life, religion shapes every story. Religious biographies open a window to the sometimes surprising influence of religion on the lives of influential people and the worlds they inhabited.

The Library of Religious Biography is a series that brings to life important figures in United States history and beyond. Grounded in careful research, these volumes link the lives of their subjects to the broader cultural contexts and religious issues that surrounded them. The authors are respected historians and recognized authorities in the historical period in which their subject lived and worked.

Marked by careful scholarship yet free of academic jargon, the books in this series are well-written narratives meant to be read and enjoyed as well as studied.

Titles include:

Emblem of Faith Untouched: A Short Life of Thomas Cranmer
by Leslie Williams

Emily Dickinson and the Art of Belief
by Roger Lundin

Damning Words: The Life and Religious Times of H. L. Mencken
by D. G. Hart

Thomas Merton and the Monastic Vision
by Lawrence S. Cunningham

Harriet Beecher Stowe: A Spiritual Life
by Nancy Koester

For a complete list of published volumes, see the back of this volume.

A Heart Lost in Wonder

The Life and Faith of Gerard Manley Hopkins

Catharine Randall

WILLIAM B. EERDMANS PUBLISHING COMPANY

GRAND RAPIDS, MICHIGAN

Wm. B. Eerdmans Publishing Co.
4035 Park East Court SE, Grand Rapids, Michigan 49546
www.eerdmans.com

Published 2020
Printed in the United States of America

26 25 24 23 22 21 20   1 2 3 4 5 6 7

ISBN 978-0-8028-7770-3

Library of Congress Cataloging-in-Publication Data

Names: Randall, Catharine, 1957– author.
Title: A heart lost in wonder : the life and faith of Gerard Manley
    Hopkins / Catharine Randall.
Description: Grand Rapids, Michigan : William B. Eerdmans Pub-
    lishing Company, 2020. | Series: Library of religious biography |
    Includes bibliographical references and index. | Summary: "A bi-
    ography of Gerard Manley Hopkins's life highlighting the role of
    his faith in his writing"—Provided by publisher.
Identifiers: LCCN 2020000845 | ISBN 9780802877703
    (paperback)
Subjects: LCSH: Hopkins, Gerard Manley, 1844–1889—Religion.
    | Poets, English—19th century—Biography. | Jesuits—En-
    gland—19th century—Biography.
Classification: LCC PR4803.H44 Z784 2020 | DDC 821/.8
    [B]—dc23
LC record available at https://lccn.loc.gov/2020000845

For the Blessed Mother

And for my beloved husband, Randall Balmer

Godhead, I adore thee fast in hiding; thou
God in these bare shapes, poor shadows, darkling now:
See, Lord, at thy service low lies here **a heart**
Lost, all **lost in wonder** at the God thou art.

—St. Thomas Aquinas, OP,
"Adoro te supplex, latens deitas,"
trans. Gerard Manley Hopkins, SJ[1]

Contents

Foreword

"THE WORLD IS charged with the grandeur of God." I was twenty-one, and had been a Christian for about ten minutes, when I first heard that line. I only dimly knew the name Gerard Manley Hopkins and hadn't read him. I'd never heard of "sprung rhythm," and I'd not yet encountered Hopkins's acute neologisms—"inscape," "instress." But like many people, I was dead stopped undone by that line from "God's Grandeur," "The world is charged with the grandeur of God." I understood I was being shown straight into things, an understanding I had again when I read the famous "Spring and Fall": "Margaret, are you grieving / Over Goldengrove unleaving?" Well, Margaret? No and yes. "It is the blight man was born for, / It is Margaret you mourn for." And then again, though with more of a smile, when someone quoted to me the opening of "Pied Beauty": "Glory be to God for dappled things." Those lines tumbled over me in my early twenties. They tumbled, and they scorched. What more needed to be said about the way the world is, and the way we are?

Still, it was some years before I sat down to properly read Hopkins, and later still before I read anything about him. How I wish I'd had Catharine Randall's *A Heart Lost in Wonder* two decades ago. I am glad to have it now.

In this biography, you will meet someone who found that his love of other people "helped him more fully to love Christ." You will meet someone to whom "trees were presences" and "birds, divine emissaries and figures of God." You will meet someone who believed that "what you look hard at seems to look hard at you," an insight that, Randall elegantly notes, "construct[ed] a relationship with objects that magicked them into subjects." Also, he adored the music of Dvořák and Purcell, and he had the outré and awkward habit of "waving a bright red handkerchief to emphasize whatever he was saying." And then comes the anguish near the end of Hopkins's life, his sense of being abandoned by God. Even if you know the story of Hopkins's late suffering, Randall's retelling will grip you. I read the last chapter, honestly, as though it were a potboiler.

Of course, there are biographies of Hopkins because of the poetry. Randall is attuned to the ways Hopkins's poetry held onto doctrinal orthodoxy yet insisted on finding divinity in the natural world and through our own experiences of human fragility—through our exhaustion and our despair. And Randall shows that Hopkins put together words as no one else has done before or since. There are few poets we can say that about, not in the way we mean it of Hopkins: he simply made words do something different. Randall draws out the "rich and innovative vocabulary, varieties of dialect, and compound words ('dapple-dawn-drawn') . . . the influence of Welsh language . . . and literature, especially its variants of *cyngahnedd* with repeating sounds—similar-sounding words with close or different meanings." In all this, Randall writes, Hopkins sought to "unfetter language from its habituated worldliness, to uncouple it from reason and sensible knowing." And he unfettered language from its habituated wordiness, too. This unfettered language is exactly how those lines I encountered twenty years ago effected their shocks: even when you've read "God's Grandeur" or "Spring and Fall" two hundred times,

Hopkins's language has the capacity to startle you into seeing things that you'd grown too accustomed to not seeing.

"Hagiography" is a term often misused. It's tossed off as a charge—the lazy but self-regarding critical thinker who accuses some other thinker of papering over the complexities of a third person's life. "Hagiography": rough edges smoothed, warts coated with face-paint.

In that sense of the word, Randall's biography of Gerard Manley Hopkins is not hagiographic. Though Randall writes with appreciation and, I believe, with love, she does not sanitize her object.

And in another sense, *A Heart Lost in Wonder* is not a hagiography: Hopkins, technically, is not a saint, so no biography of him could be "a saint's life."

Yet I propose that this biography unfolds Hopkins as a saint of sorts. A saint has set apart, or allowed God to set apart, some aspect of his life for peculiarly intimate participation with God. Hopkins was set apart as a priest, but his keenest and weirdest setting apart was in and by the sonnets and the sprung rhythm and all the light metaphors and "her wild hollow hoarlight hung" and "I wake and feel the fell of dark, not day."

One of my favorite moments in this biography comes early on, when Randall suggests we might think of a Hopkins poem as a "sacramental." Sacramentals, in the Roman Catholic lexicon (here, following Randall, I quote the catechism), "prepare us to receive grace and dispose us to cooperate with it." Blessings are sacramentals, as is the sign of the cross, a saint's medal, beeswax candles, your grandmother's rosary. It is right to think of "Pied Beauty" and "God's Grandeur" and Hopkins's late despairing poems in just this way—preparing us to receive grace, disposing us to cooperate with it.

The point of hagiography is not blunt emulation—few of us

will read *A Heart Lost in Wonder*, or indeed Hopkins himself, and take up writing verse. Rather, saints deepen our questions, and *A Heart Lost in Wonder* is a hagiography insofar as the experience of looking at Hopkins's faithfulness moves us to ask about our own.

Lauren F. Winner
May 7, 2020

Preface

GERARD MANLEY HOPKINS was born July 28, 1844, in Stratford, England, and died June 8, 1889, in Dublin, Ireland. During his lifetime he was well connected and in dialogue with many of the major artistic figures of the late nineteenth century: Tennyson, Ruskin, Turner, Bridges, Yeats. After his life, he became an unexpected literary phenomenon, admired posthumously by many of the great modernist writers: Joyce, Eliot, Auden. Gerard was a polymath, priest, and poet, a product of his time, the Victorian era, and he embodied a paradox: one of today's best-known and beloved poets, he was never published during his own lifetime and was often misunderstood in his own day and age. The way in which his poetry has been approached is also somewhat paradoxical, in that, although he was a man for whom religious vocation was true and strong, many readers do not discern or grasp the spiritual richness of his work.[1] He was, for many reasons, a multifaceted and fascinating figure, and although his life was brief, his influence and his accomplishments were numerous and abiding.[2]

A Heart Lost in Wonder provides perspective on the life and work of Gerard Manley Hopkins through a complementary religious and literary interpretation. The biography describes and contextualizes the experiences of Gerard's intense, textured life, with interest often tilted in the direction of religion and art—both those of his era and his own personally. As the eminent Jesuit theologian Hans Urs von Balthasar has argued, "the priest, the theologian and the poet in Hopkins are not to be separated. Despite all the obvious tension, any attempt to find inner contradictions in him [is] a radical misunderstanding." This biography pays attention to the dual theological and aesthetic aspects commended by von Balthasar in relation to Gerard's poetry: "the unprecedented character of Hopkins' language is a theological phenomenon and can be understood only in this way."[3]

Gerard's life is a narrative, which unfolds for the most part chronologically, in which his own questions and responses frame the reader's experience. Gerard's voice is facilitated in telling his own story, through his prose and poetical writings, and as a creature of his Victorian context. A somewhat unusual aspect of this biography that calls for clarification is that it is my own construction of Hopkins's life; I hope it is perceived in a more popular way than in a scholarly manner. To that end, I have used quotations in a holistic way: with the understanding that all aspects of a person's life, and literary production, are interconnected and mutually informing. Pathways may be perceived after the fact; epiphanies occur; corrections of course ensue. As a result, when it appeared helpful or enlightening, at times I have quoted, out of chronological order, insights that Hopkins may have had at a later date about an earlier event, or earlier awarenesses that appear in retrospect to be foreshadowings of something to come. I hoped thereby to achieve a "you are there" feeling for the reader, a face-to-face encounter with my portrait, at least, of Hopkins—an interpretive biography, a life viewed through the prism of theology. I sought to write a biography that takes his theology seriously—because he took it seriously.

Gerard experienced great highs and lows, sudden epiphanies and conversions, dramatic changes of heart, periods of exultation and of abiding sorrow and spiritual aridity. These states enrich his writing and our experience of reading it. They may embody what Gerard termed "selfness": in this case, his own.[4] Rather than a neurosis or a pathology, these quicksilver changes of mood are an innate constitutional response: simply who Gerard was, how he experienced the world, and how he apprehended God.

The biography begins with a brief section entitled "Alpha," and it concludes with an equally brief section entitled "Omega," the two symbolizing Gerard's self-chosen insertion of his life and work within the will of God or, as he put it, "Christ *being* me and me being Christ."[5]

"Preparation" takes Gerard through a childhood surrounded by family and steeped in the natural world, his early schooling, and his Oxford years. Then, he developed his love for drawing and music, and above all for nature, demonstrating an interest, typical of many in the Victorian era, in collecting oddities and things of beauty. He admired the paintings of the Pre-Raphaelite Brotherhood, especially those of Dante Gabriel Rossetti. And he studied classics, philosophy, mathematics, and many other subjects and was influenced by the coaching of Walter Pater and Benjamin Jowett, as well as the theories and sketching of John Ruskin. While a student at Oxford, Gerard also had what appears to have been a life-changing encounter with the charismatic and hyper-religious Digby Dolben—a falling into love that may have made Christ knowable to Gerard in an embodied way that Gerard's Anglican confessor would condemn as blasphemous. At Oxford, Gerard became disenchanted with the Tractarianism prevailing in Anglicanism at the time, even given his friendship with Edward Pusey, last high priest of the Oxford Movement. Writing poetry copiously at the time, Gerard made a decision to forsake poetry and art in order to sacrifice these gifts to God by becoming a priest.

His conversion and vocation were fueled by his hero worship of, and transformative interview with, John Henry Newman. Gerard yearned for a pure and original form of Catholicism, a truth he could profess with passion. Roman Catholicism would, for him, surpass the High Church Anglicanism in which he had been reared: an Anglicanism replete with vestments and liturgy and incense but practiced more as a somewhat lip-service state religion. All these contacts and experiences, viewed through Gerard's correspondence, journal entries, poetry, and prose, are considered as formative influences on the man Gerard was to become.

"Dedication," chapter 2, moves Gerard into the Roman Catholic fold, sees him embrace a vocation as a Jesuit priest, and details his formation in the Society of Jesus. It examines the significance of Gerard's "bonfire of vanities," what he himself referred to, only half in jest, as his "slaughter of the innocents" in which he burned all but some fragments of poetry earlier sent to, and conserved by, friends such as Robert Bridges.[6] Gerard completed seven years of his Jesuit novitiate and postulancy and was subsequently ordained.

During his theologate, or third year of study, he had a serendipitous encounter—to his mind, if not to that of many of his Jesuit superiors, who were caught up in the current revival of neo-scholasticism after Leo III's papal bull *Aeternis Patris* (1879) emphasizing the thought of Thomas Aquinas—with the theology of Duns Scotus.[7] Gerard's reading of Scotus provided a way for him to exalt nature in all its quirks and particularities as the privileged revelation of God. Gerard interprets Scotus's philosophy as a "thingness" (Scotus called it something approximating "selfness") of each object, each possessing its "inscape," which Gerard evoked, for example, in "all things counter, original, spáre, strange," "dappled," "brinded," "fickle, frecklèd."[8] This very particular view of the self communicates via its "instress" to all of creation, which in turn plays a role ("counterstress") in responding to that movement.

"Illumination" fleshes out an understanding of joint theological and literary production as a potential path to sanctity for Gerard, incorporating as illustrations original and detailed readings of some of his most significant poems. Excerpts and snippets of Gerard's journals pose as forerunners or prototypes of verse that he later penned, drawing directly on his prose descriptions, thus writing his life experience into his literary web. Gerard experiences a sort of epiphany concerning the conjoining of his Roman Catholic sacramental theology, its immanent aspect, and his love for nature. Indeed, Gerard may have been working toward an understanding of his poetry not as sacrament (as has been argued elsewhere)[9] but rather as what the Roman Catholic catechism calls a "sacramental": a special action, or a more crafted or constructed medium (such as a prayer, or telling one's rosary beads, or perhaps a poem), by which one may avail oneself of divine grace.[10]

Gerard's priestly vocation is set in motion as he begins to be sent out, as is the Jesuit custom, to numerous clergy postings, particularly in the dreary northern industrial cities, to the Irish in the slums of Liverpool, as well as a short stint serving in Oxford. Deprived of his beloved countryside rambles and rural wonders, Gerard starts to feel the stirrings of the dire depression that will haunt the rest of his brief life. His teaching posts throughout England, Ireland, and Wales and his preaching among the urban poor—not a notable success, since his idiom was too elevated and his mannerisms distinctly peculiar—all have an effect on his growing need to resume writing poetry. He does not actually renew his poetic endeavors, however, until his superior requests that he commemorate the contemporary tragedy of the sinking of the *Deutschland* with all souls aboard, more than a quarter of whom perished. The *Deutschland* had been sheltering nuns fleeing persecution in Germany. Along with poetic production, Gerard also begins work on an annotation of Ignatius of Loyola's *Spiritual Exercises*, whose strategy for meditation will have an influence on Gerard's poetry. *The Spiritual Exercises*, with its sensorial techniques of visualization and "memory theatres," or contemplative practice of selected scriptural scenarios, provides a framework for Gerard's interaction with the world around him and for his development of theological and aesthetic understanding.

"Desolation," chapter 4, shows the specter of depression and self-loathing becoming a near-constant presence, stalking Gerard's daily grind of duties in Dublin, where he was professor and grader for an endless round of university examinations. Gerard experiences devastating alienation, depression, and isolation in Dublin, where he writes "the terrible sonnets" (as his worried friends termed them), his most powerful yet most baleful poetry ever, a sort of poetic acting-out of a death wish. God, always so close to Gerard in the warp and woof of the world, its texture and creative tumult, seems now to have abandoned him, is withdrawn, appears intentionally vengeful.

Yet there is another revelation or coming-to-terms toward the end of Gerard's life, when he reorients his interpretation of the psychic and spiritual suffering he has undergone, understanding this eventually as a salubrious trial, akin to the refiner's fire. And then the sudden, untimely death from typhoid fever—his short, intense life compressed like a brilliant, compacted diamond, with his poems only appearing posthumously through the midwifery of his lifelong friend who was to become poet laureate, Robert Bridges.

A Heart Lost in Wonder: The Life and Faith of Gerard Manley Hopkins understands Gerard's life and experiences through conversations with family, mentors, friends, and other poets preserved in correspondence. It also discusses the prevailing artistic and literary influences of the day—what Gerard takes from them, his differences with them, as well as how he theorizes these changes. This portrait of Gerard is delineated with reference to the changing contexts of the increasing industrialization of England, the grim plight of the working poor to whom Gerard was sent, debates over Irish nationalism, the rise of socialism, Darwinism, philosophical materialism, and atomism. Tensions appear in Gerard's psyche between self-expression and obedience, literary production as contrasted with the ideal of spiritual "poverty," and what comes to be his ultimate perception of vocation.

Gerard's highly personal philosophical appropriation of Franciscan theology, especially that of Duns Scotus, has a theologically and literarily formative effect on him. Gerard's poetry is informed by his religious sentiment, while his spiritual fervor is stoked and expressed by his poetic sensibility. A sensualist who best perceives the world of senses spiritually, he is a spiritual sensitive who most strongly understands the Spirit through the senses in what seems a form of poetic synesthesia, or way of experiencing multisensory input simultaneously. In this way, Gerard embodies an apparent paradox that ultimately is revealed not as dichotomy or polarity but rather as fullness, completion, presence. He seeks a verbal, imaged bridge between grace and nature, man and God, and in his striving after this goal, he himself unwittingly forms a bridge between the Romantic poets of the Victorian age and the modernist poets who were to follow.

Gerard invents his own vocabulary—a set of neologisms and the occasional revival of archaisms—to convey his rationale for his theological and literary juxtapositions: "inscape" and "instress" display both psychological and spiritual phenomena. In Gerard's innovative, demanding use of poetic language, he acutely reworks the rhythm of English inflections and speech, which had been influenced by Norman roots in which there are customarily two or three groups of syllables, with the stressed syllable always falling on the same one: Gerard calls this "running rhythm." A linguistic purist, Gerard learned Old English and became fascinated with Anglo-Saxon, especially *Beowulf*, in which he found "feet" with a varying number of syllables (one to four per foot), with stress always on the first: Gerard uses this in what he calls "sprung rhythm."

Primal and authentic, sprung rhythm offers a way to escape the constraints of running rhythm, which had, according to Gerard, the effect of making poetry "same and tame." In this, Gerard anticipates free verse and is now seen as a modernist precursor.

Further, he deploys a rich and innovative vocabulary, varieties of dialect, and compound words ("dapple-dawn-drawn"), sometimes with a hyphen, sometimes without, to communicate the intensely intimate relationship of poet to his image; he also uses much alliteration, assonance, onomatopoeia, end and internal rhyme. The influence of Welsh language, in which he received tutoring from a Miss Susannah Jones, and literature, especially its variants of *cyngahnedd* with repeating sounds—similar-sounding words with close or different meanings—makes his poetry musical; his poetry is best read aloud, sounded like music. Sprung rhythm could be interpreted in the way a prisoner might be "sprung" from a jail, as the soul is released from its "bone-house"; understanding in a deeply sacramental way the Word made flesh, Gerard seeks to unfetter language from its habituated worldliness, to uncouple it from reason and sensible knowing. Yet he also believes poetry should reflect actual rhythms and speech patterns—and this contradicts Romantic poetic practice. Idiosyncratically, he may introduce a hyphen, or a third term, a compound word, a pause, an ejaculation to express the Word extricating itself from word while also still expressing itself in and through matter.

Gerard combined what he had learned from Walter Pater at university, and later from the work of John Ruskin, with what he found in Scotus as theological justification for his aesthetic sensibility. While Aquinas had asserted that "grace builds upon nature," Scotus, kindred to Gerard's temperament, could be said to show that "grace already inhabits nature": the quiddity of each individual phenomenon displays immanence of the divine. Gerard's concern for detail, exactitude, and beauty in his descriptions of nature leads him to an equally fine and meticulous attention to the words that speak their thingness, just as the Logos speaks the world into being. For example, elucidating his images for how the world is ablaze with the grandeur of God, describing it like "shook foil," Gerard clarifies scrupulously: "I mean foil in its sense of leaf or tinsel, and no other word whatever will give the effect I want. Shaken goldfoil gives off broad glares like sheet lightning and also, and this is true of nothing else, owing to its zigzag dints and creasings and network of small many cornered facets, a sort of fork lightning too."[11]

For Gerard, it is essential that Primal Voice be enabled to burst through the matter of human word. This is a complex and hard thought: Gerard evokes the gospel when Christ says, "Let those who have eyes to see, see, and those who have ears to hear, hear," and likens himself to Christ on the road to Emmaus, who, undiscerned in his risen flesh by the disciples he is accompanying along the road, leaves them at the same time he becomes sacramentally known to them in the breaking of the bread when they sit down, road-weary, at table to eat. Gerard speaks to his dearest friends and interlocutors, poignantly saying, "It is plain I must go no further on this road; if you [Bridges] and he [Dixon] cannot understand me, who will?"[12]

A theophanist, or one who perceives manifestations of the divine in forms that are visible but need not be tangible or material, Gerard develops a profoundly sacramental understanding of God in Christ and of Christ in matter, in primal matter and motion even before the world began, in a way that anticipates the radical "environmental" theology of Teilhard de Chardin. Working through Scotus's theology that the sacrifice of the Son was God's first thought of the world, Gerard asserts that for this victim to be a true and full victim, it must be incarnational, enfleshed in matter. But, in Gerard's theophanic understanding, we may not actually see or touch him, but by glancing obliquely, as it were, at and through matter, we may discern aspects of him in all entities and circumstances. Hence the exquisite significance that Gerard gives to each creature. He views nature sacramentally: "I know the beauty of Our Lord by it," Gerard exclaims, enthralled by the beauty of a bluebell growing in a meadow.[13] In this way, writing becomes a means of expressing theology and the epiphanies that daily occur in ordinary reality.[14] Reading also many of the patristic writers, particularly the Eastern fathers, Gerard has a notion of what they termed "the Cosmic Christ"—as evidenced also by his proto-environmental sentiments and his opposition, as in the poem "Binsey Poplars," to the felling of trees in particular.[15]

"The Windhover," probably Gerard's best-known poem, is, by several accounts, the "most read" poem in the English language. Ironically, given how grading exams exhausted Gerard and wore out his health, "The Windhover" is also one of the most-assigned poems to examinations; most Oxford students will have been graded on their competency in parsing its meaning. Virtually any modern-day Roman Catholic with an interest in things literary will own a copy of Gerard's poems—this is ironic, as the Society of Jesus did not allow the publication of any of the poems that Gerard submitted for their approval. The famous contemporary theologian and public figure who at times tours with the Dalai Lama, Father Richard Rohr, a Franciscan, used Gerard's poetry as the inspiration, and title, of one of his most influential volumes of self-help theology, *Immortal Diamond*—this, too, is ironic, since Gerard's own peers often regarded him as anything but competent, useful, or practical. Even his dear friend Bridges damned Gerard with faint praise upon his death, expressing to his correspondent Canon Dixon, "how much worse [his death] would have been had his promise or performance been more splendid,"[16] and implied, when he published the first, posthumous, edition of Gerard's poetry in 1918, that his discomfort with its quirks had restrained him from issuing the collection earlier.

The most immediately compelling argument for rereading Gerard Manley Hopkins in this day and time may be the stunning revelation by the British government on November 1, 2018, that a spectacular bequest had been made to the Bodleian Library in Oxford. Entitled the "Bridges Archive," it was acquired from the estate of Robert Bridges's grandson, Thomas Edward Bridges, second Baron Bridges. The archive comprises dozens of boxes in which, along with Poet Laureate Bridges's papers and letters from W. B. Yeats, Prime Minister Herbert Asquith, and many other prominent contemporary figures, can be found Gerard's "A" manuscript of seventy-four of his poems in his own hand-writing, hitherto thought destroyed or forever missing. It is a nearly complete collection of Gerard's poems, bound together by Bridges, some of which were emended by Bridges in red ink.[17]

It just may be that our present day and age is, in fact, Gerard's best audience. Perhaps *we* are those with eyes to see and ears to hear, who will accompany Gerard further on his road. In a strange, paradoxical way that Gerard himself surely could never have anticipated, readers of the present day are often people more willing to perceive divinity in the numinous, in nature, in art. We are readers more likely to deem ourselves "mystic" or "spiritual" than religious or "creedal"; readers more inclined to trust experience over doctrine; we are lovers of poetry as Presence, readers with historical curiosity and an interest in delving into the more personal portrait of, and less scholarly take on, the life and thought of the man behind this poetry. While Gerard was in every way utterly orthodox in his dogma and submitted willingly and obediently to the authority of the Roman Catholic hierarchy and of his Jesuit superiors, he lifts up experience as a valued means of apprehending the divine, yet also never seeks to contradict doctrine. It is perhaps that very creative tension that accounts for why some of his poetry is, ultimately, so compelling.

A Heart Lost in Wonder: The Life and Faith of Gerard Manley Hopkins offers an accessible, reader-friendly version of Gerard's life and work. And I believe this is what Gerard himself hopes for: this convoluted, complex, creative man, little understood in his own time, so very formative for the modernist poets, such a transformational figure in so many ways yet acknowledged so very belatedly, is now no longer available only to the Oxford don. He is now also available to Gerard's own poetic persona, whom he calls Jack: "every man Jack."

Alpha: Things Seen and Unseen

Or what is else? There is your world within. [1]

THE WIDE WORLD lay without—with its broad sweeps of lawn and stretches of meadows, its bowling greens and tussocky hills— but the world also lay within, the child found. In the hothouse Victorian front parlor of Hampstead Heath, its curtains drawn against the light, collectors' boxes, pin cases of butterflies, and antimacassars cluttering the dark, oversized furniture, the boy grew interiorly. He discovered that he could reach for experience by glancing out the window, by walking down a lane, by skipping over the bricks in the garden and throwing pebbles in the pond. He found there "life, this wildworth blown so sweet":[2] flashes of color, fragments of detail, shimmering of light, glimmers of life proceeding in broad daylight yet oddly undercover, unheeded by most. He discerned a glory in nature, and this brought him joy. He loved small things and cherished color, pattern, prism, ley lines, and order. He became convinced of mystery, an interpreter of signs. Reared a High Church Anglican accustomed to liturgical processions, vestments, and incense, his creed a belief in "all things seen and unseen," the boy became the decipherer of cosmic code. And in this way he learned a technique for enhancing his life sensually. The world of the senses became the high road to the world of the spirit.

By nature quiet and contemplative, the small boy lived sur-

rounded by women and a clutch of siblings. His father, a somewhat distant man and a disciplinarian, was often not at home, but
his mother, and his aunt Annie, in particular, encouraged Gerard
to draw and paint and sing and mount theatrical dramas and play
musical instruments. His aunt Maria taught him to sketch; his
uncle George Giberne introduced the boy to the techniques of
photography.

A lover of hobbies, as small boys often are, he had the inclinations of a tinkerer. Perhaps inherited from his father, a ship's ad-
juster, was a need for order and accounting and careful technique
in execution. He built structures and made cobbled streets and
thatched houses. A job worth doing was worth doing well. All the
trades—carpentry, shoemaking, fishing—fascinated him with
their tackle and their precision, their unique vocabulary and practical terminology. The special words had a taste on his tongue.

And he had the soul of a romantic. Cosseted among the horse-
hair stuffed sofas and vases filled with imperial palms, he yearned
for beauty. What he saw of it intoxicated him—the bright blue of a
caged parakeet, an elaborate tapestry hung in the entryway, a print of
Sir Galahad, fine-featured, noble, strong. He read Keats early on.

When he went out of doors, he breathed a freer air. He saw
signs and wonders, swaths of the sky, the spirit in the swoop of a
hawk's wing, the sparkle of color in a river rock. On visits to his
maternal grandparents, the Smiths, he breathed in the country
air, and he reveled in family trips to the Isle of Wight. He saw
there was another, wider world, and he taught himself to bring it
within. All was beauty—the wide world and the world within.

And there he learned to live more richly. He schooled himself
in observation of the finest delineation of all that he saw. He set
himself the task of describing as intricately and accurately as he
could. He came to believe that if he could find the exact word,
the proper phrase, to evoke the most intimate life of what he saw,
he could incorporate it. It would become a part of him. The small
boy was developing a sacramental understanding of the world.

He was master of mysteries! He saw, beyond "the veil that covers mysteries . . . / the mystery of those Things . . . / the common earth and air / Were limn'd about with radiance rare," as he was to claim in one of his earliest, youthful poems written when he was eighteen years old.[3]

He was a beautiful little child, shorter in stature than most boys his age, elfin almost in appearance, his deep-set, huge hazel eyes peering out bravely from a thick fringe of light brown lashes, his high forehead betokening unusual intelligence.[4] He had a finely chiseled mouth, a cleft chin, and a long nose. His fine hair feathered gently around his large ears, but he had a most stubborn set to his jaw. He was willful and fanciful and utterly charming. He early learned to swim, and he loved to take country rambles, armed with a stout stick.

When he was lonely or left out of games for lack of athletic prowess or because of his small size, he could go to his enchanted world and there soak himself in its immediacy and beauty and powerful simplicity. From the parlor window, the wide world unscrolled itself before his gaze: God's book for Gerard to view and read, and even he thought it his role to decode. And he gazed bemusedly, carefully, absorbing every detail of each creature that darted past, the crenellations of furled leaves and the scattering of snow on garden pebble walks.

He was a shy child, but also mischievous and witty. His younger siblings adored him, swarming about him with requests for invented doggerel, tossed-off limericks, funny poems, staged plays. The family loved to play charades. They amiably vied to cap each other's puns. Language, with its richness and complexity, even its plastic ambiguity, was a field he early reveled in. Gerard costumed himself and his siblings, using felt and scraps from his aunt's sewing basket, paints from her, too, for she was an accomplished watercolorist and encouraged him to become one as well, and tinsel and foil from birthday presents and Christmas wrappings—fashioning identities for a new, invented world.

Theater and music and painting became mediums for Gerard to enter into more of the world's mysteries. Anglican ritual, steeped in sounds, smells, and ritual staging, similarly lured him with a promise of beauty, truth, and a deeper world beyond. Child of devout churchgoers who cherished their religion as much as their Englishness, Gerard viewed the green countryside as a manifestation of the glory of God. The small boy scrutinized objects more than he attended to people, communed with inanimate objects and animate creatures rather than engage in extensive eye contact with adults. When he sketched in his pocket sketchbooks, he rarely drew people. When he did, they had no clear facial delineations. Yet he spent hours capturing every shadow and indentation of a cunningly shaped rock and sketched every feather of a fledgling sparrow.

He was easily drawn to beauty of all kinds, especially that of the natural world, but also to the well-ordered lineaments of a neighbor's child, the symmetrical golden beauty of hay bales dotting a pasture, the changes of sea and sand and stars and sky. In autumn, the world seemed truly ablaze with the grandeur of God, as leaves gashed gold-vermilion. Although the Hopkins's home was close to Cambridge, not really in the country but rather nestled in a village, Gerard seems early to have craved access to nature.

Later, when he was sent away to school, this predisposition for harmony and order and beauty would find justification in Platonic philosophy. What was above was ideal and absolute, yet could be found here below in fractured form. He could set shattered shards of beauty in savant arrangements and re-create wholeness. As a child, this had been his practice, however unconscious and unintentional it may have been. As an adult, it became his discipline and his devotion, his calling and his offering.

He was a perfectionist even as a child. Things had to be just so—or he would fly into a fury. Lead soldiers must stand straight, all in a line. His first year at school, he took a vow to endure an entire month without drinking any water. His tongue turned black, but he persevered for twenty-one days until an alarmed schoolmate told on him and the schoolmaster thrashed Gerard for bizarre and dangerous behavior. This was all part and parcel of Gerard's ascesis—his yearning after perfection and beauty and his self-dedication. For him, clearly, ascesis and aesthetics were intertwined. Beauty could not exist without order and arrangement and framework; symmetry was discernible throughout nature as a signpost to its divine origin. And he was its sacerdos—special reader of those sacred signs.

CHAPTER 1

PREPARATION

Think of an opening page illuminèd
With the ready azure and high carmine:—think. [1]

GERARD MANLEY HOPKINS was born into a talented and, in many respects, quite eccentric family on July 28, 1844, in Stratford in Essex. His father, Manley Hopkins (1818–1897), and his mother, Kate (1821–1920), had nine children. Kate's father, a medical doctor, had been a student of the poet Keats, and Gerard's mother admired Keats's work very much, sharing that enthusiasm with her eldest son. One of her distant relatives had been a Gainsborough, and Kate always thought her love for art derived from this kinship. She loved music, painting, languages—especially excelling at German—and poetry—the trinity of interests that was to shape so much of Gerard's life. Gerard grew up petted by family influences, especially those of his mother and his father's sister, Annie. They encouraged him to express himself artistically and theatrically, and he seems to have derived from their nurture a sense of great confidence in his ability to succeed in all his endeavors. One of Gerard's younger brothers, Arthur, was a confidant and companion, joining in a lifelong love for art galleries and excursions to museums.

Eventually, his mother became a sort of mediator between her fastidious and fanciful son and his brusque and demanding father, who was not pleased by Gerard's sensitive nature. Himself not at a loss for confidence, even brashness, Manley published poetry and wrote a novel, but he also wrote books on insurance adjusting, primarily for the maritime trade, and had published a history of Hawaii, which he had never visited. He was later appointed consul to Hawaii, where he enjoyed a good diplomatic relationship with King Kamehameha's nephew, with whom Manley's brother, the family black sheep Charles (nicknamed Polly), had struck up a somewhat controversial friendship while living in a *ménage à trois* in Hawaii. Manley himself was an immensely upstanding and relentless moralizer, decrying homosexuality, eschewing Roman Catholicism as a religious aberration tainted with disloyalty to the nation, derogating Irish immigrants, expressing himself abundantly on every subject.[2]

Manley took his family to church regularly, and he became warden of St. John's Anglican Church when they moved to Oak Hill Park. He also served as rector of the church school, penning uplifting moralizing tracts for the school's publication. Every evening, he expected the entire family to join in family prayers. The family, moderately High Church, reading Scripture regularly and also practicing a sacramental piety, lived in a devout atmosphere. This piety had an effect: most of the offspring remained religious, and Gerard's sister, Millicent, became an Anglican nun. When Manley served as consul to Hawaii, he worked with the bishop of Oxford, Samuel Wilberforce, appointing High Churchmen to the position of bishop of Hawaii.

Manley sent Gerard to Highgate School at the age of ten. The school was aptly the father's choice; Gerard hated it for its austere and brutal nature. The headmaster was renowned for his skill with the whip. Gerard could have felt an affinity with David Copperfield, another small and brutalized boy, the protagonist in the Dickens novel beloved by the Hopkins family. Most of his time there Gerard was a boarder, though he was briefly a day student. Despite the headmaster's disciplinary overzealousness, Highgate provided Gerard with some important early influences and training. The Highgate headmaster, Dr. John Dyne, employed the pedagogical technique of teaching correct English by having his students translate the classics, focusing thereby on the complexities of grammar and the multivalences of vocabulary, and the talented Richard Watson Dixon, friend and one of the storied Pre-Raphaelite poets whom Gerard so much admired, was a junior master while Gerard was a student there.[3] At Highgate, Gerard won many prizes, including a prize for poetry in 1860, which led to him being sent up to Oxford three years later. He was very popular with the other boys for his winsome ways and quick wit, earning himself many affectionate and silly nicknames, such as "Skin" (an anagram of the latter part of his surname). He seethed and simmered with rebelliousness at the innumerable school rules but generally managed to steer clear of confrontation, preferring to mock his targets verbally and with caricature behind their backs. He struck up many affectionate relationships. Contemporary portrait shots show him leaning warmly on a friend's arm, draping himself companionably over the back of a lawn chair in which another friend sat, bedecked with a boater; always diminutive and almost dwarfed by his peers, Gerard nonetheless took center stage habitually.

This social ease continued when he went up to Oxford in April of 1863. Gerard took rooms in Balliol College, promptly pinning as wallpaper unframed portraits of all his heroes, among them Dürer, Raphael, some Pre-Raphaelite painters, as well as the poets Tennyson and Keats, and inviting many friends to his lodgings for tea. Gerard valued good looks, a strong ethical sensibility, and intelligence in his male friends. At Oxford, accompanied invariably by a friend, he rowed, canoed, swam, and took leisurely walks over the college grounds and out into the long green swaths of meadow beyond.

Gerard thought widely and deeply; he had passions, those that were intellectual generally outlasting the brief and numerous crushes he experienced (primarily his self-avowed "pashes" on curly-headed Magdalen College choristers). Gerard studied Greek and Latin, read poetry, and joined in discussions of his preferred topics, architecture and painting. He admired Ruskin

and Rossetti. He had a penchant for things medieval, the Holy
Grail and the Knights of the Round Table, and admired oriel
windows and flying buttresses, which he sketched in his many
sketchbooks. In the company of friends, Gerard rambled around
the local country roads, seeking out antique sites and old churches
to explore.

Gerard's career at Balliol College, Oxford, 1863–1867, was
not an immediately unmitigated academic success. Although
he eventually did receive the scholarship for which he had applied, he did not pass its first set of qualifying exams. He was
unhappy and disoriented there at first, and so did not buckle
down, which nearly cost him the scholarship. However, while
at Oxford, Gerard studied with many first-rate scholars, hearing
firsthand widely differing perspectives on religion and theology
and how these affected the daily life of undergraduates. Among
them was Gerard's tutor for Greats, the redoubtable Benjamin
Jowett, Regius Professor of Greek, who at the time was notorious
for his liberal religious views. Edward Bouverie Pusey, an oppo-
nent of Jowett's, also had an influence on Gerard. Pusey's position
contradicted that of Jowett; Pusey fought against what he saw as
the pernicious effect of Enlightenment rationalism on Oxford
undergraduates, and he tried to counter this trend by writing
an "eirenicon" in which he showed the historic similarity of the
Church of England to the Roman Catholic Church. Oxford was
a Church of England school, as were all English universities by
law, and had only recently begun, in 1863, in a few colleges (of
which Balliol was one), to admit Roman Catholics for study.
All students, nonetheless, were still required to subscribe to the
official Church of England theology, the Thirty-Nine Articles.
Pusey's position as a prominent neo-Tractarian, a leader in the
Oxford Anglo-Catholic movement, was highly controversial.
The Tractarian Movement, an attempt to counter what was
deemed an "Anglican apostasy" or disaffection from, or national
ignorance concerning, the Church of England, had begun thirty

years before Gerard entered Oxford and was still widely debated. Gerard was soon to enter the fray, choosing one of Pusey's confreres, the young Anglo-Catholic theologian Henry Parry Liddon, to be his regular confessor, a selection that offered a good clue to Gerard's developing religious sensibilities.[4]

Gerard was also choosing up sides on issues that mattered to him. As a second-year student at Oxford, Gerard joined a society in which students debated controversial issues by penning essays. Gerard very publicly took a stand against Pater—essayist, literary figure, Renaissance scholar, and art critic who was the literary lion of a select coterie of Oxford undergraduates—who had denied the existence of life after death. Pater was an anti-Christian, exponent of a belief termed "Neology," who claimed that beauty—and life—needed no divine justification; all that mattered was intensity of feeling toward perception. But, increasingly, Gerard, though admiring Pater as a scholar, could not agree. Gerard continued to apply Pater's teachings, akin to Ruskin's in asserting the mandate of a well-trained and discerning eye for detail in moving from the general to the particular in nature, as well as in the intellectual apprehension of concepts.

In the final term of his second year at Oxford, with Pater's coaching, Gerard began to develop a high and exalted Platonic conception of poetic form. As an underclassman, even prior to coaching with Pater, Gerard had already elaborated his own tripartite poetic theory: what was commonly called poetry he deemed pedestrian; what sometimes soared but could not sustain the stress of glory he termed Parnassian; his ideal and aim were "poetry proper, language of inspiration . . . language of the sacred *Plain*, Delphic."[5] True poetry, Gerard assessed, had an oracular, prophetic function. It stood shoulder to shoulder with the gods; it scrutinized the heavens; true poetry was sublime beauty, and Gerard aspired to this. His poetic theory closely cousined his theological inclinations.[6] All that was best and brightest was to be aimed at; the dross should drop behind.

Gerard loved Oxford. As would be the case with other places crucial to him in his spiritual development, notably parts of Wales, he entertained a sense of intimate relationship with it. He strolled around its grounds with a proprietary sense, calling Oxford "my park, my pleasaunce," alluding to its bell towers and rose windows with pride and a hint of lover's possessiveness: "all mine, yet common to my every peer," Oxford was more fully his, he claimed, because "I . . . set the same to pen."[7] Writing was becoming for him a strategy for knowing, naming, appropriating, claiming. Context was a blanket he wrapped himself in; the details of environs were claim stakes to his mastery.

When Gerard was not studying or roistering about, he was beginning to attend to theology. By his second year at Oxford, his letters, addressed dutifully to both parents but progressively assuming a different and distinct voice and style for each correspondent,[8] began to take up theological issues. His Anglican background was being tested against the zeitgeist of the day, for the Oxford community was Liberal, or Broad Church. A summary sketch of the theological battle lines would show that Jowett's stance was applauded; in general, that of Pusey—High Church—was officially not encouraged.

Until very recently, and due to the influence of John Henry Newman, who was also to play such a major role in Gerard's life, there had been no Roman Catholic universities in England. Ever since the Catholic Church had sought to undermine the English monarchy on behalf of the pope during the English Reformation and recusant period, Englishmen had perceived Catholicism as unpatriotic and a threat to their way of life. Oxford was no exception. Students were required to attend Anglican chapel; the piety of the masters was scrutinized; and, as noted, until a very recent date, one could not enroll in or graduate from Oxford unless one were Anglican. But this was a new sort of Anglicanism to Gerard, who was more accustomed to the high liturgy and elaborate vestments of High Church Anglicanism—the English

Church as it had been when it separated from Rome, retaining Roman customs but abandoning allegiance to the papacy.

Broad Church was more Protestant in its focus on Scripture, with less attention paid to sacramental observance. The Oxford dons viewed creeds and dogmas as much less significant than individual experience of religion, and this experiential emphasis also led them to be receptive to Darwinian views, controversial at the time in other church circles. Gerard's house master at Balliol College, Robert Scott, gave a lecture in the University Lecture Series on the Pauline epistles, advocating a more literal interpretation of them, in line with traditional piety.[9] Demonstrating how divisively drawn the theological adherences were, Scott was directly responsible for the defeat by one vote of Jowett when he sought to become Balliol house master. Jowett, Regius Professor of Greek, was a prominent member of the Broad Church faction. In 1860, he contributed a controversial essay to the prestigious publication *Essays and Reviews*. Here, alongside the essays of six other Anglican academics, Jowett argued for a de-privileging of the Bible's status; it should be read like anything else, and higher criticism should be applied to it. His thought also appeared sympathetic to Darwinian theory of evolution in *Origin of Species* (1859).

For the Broad Church party, being English and being Anglican were virtually one and the same; Balliol College, which produced so many leading statesmen and government functionaries, ensured that church and state retained their traditional marriage and mutually reinforcing norms. But Broad Church theology seemed diluted and rather prosaic to Gerard's poetical mind, and its jettisoning of most creeds seemed crudely ahistorical and unphilosophical to him. Gerard began to toy with the idea of returning to the ancient church, to Roman Catholicism. At the very least, he began to practice regularly a very high, or Anglo-Catholic, form of piety, making auricular confession every three months as recommended by his confessor, keeping a journal in which he scrupulously noted his daily sins,[10] as the High Church party urged young men to do, and eventually, after his conversion in 1866, attending early morning mass at Blackfriars, the Dominican chapel at Oxford. High Church piety depended on—indeed, elevated to a very high status—the intermediary function of a priest, who was necessary to hear confession and offer absolution and to celebrate the miracle of transubstantiation, the transformation of the wafer and wine into the body and blood of Christ. But such beliefs were scoffed at by the preachers of the Broad Church party, who exhorted that Christ alone was the mediator, sufficient for all, and that High Church observances were papistical extravagances for a coterie of effete young men to swoon over.

Many of Gerard's associates at Oxford disagreed with him, and friendships, such as that with Bridges, which would deepen in later years, foundered over religious differences. Bridges was the stepson of an Anglican clergyman. Although he had been a regular churchgoer and a choirboy, Bridges now focused on studies in Greats in Arts and Letters. He found Broad Church theology more lenient and less dramatic than High Church; his personality was not drawn to extremes or to the need to espouse a position ardently and to express devotion, as was Gerard's. Bridges reasoned with Gerard and, although he never formally left the Church of England, became increasingly agnostic. Bridges, unlike Gerard (one of whose Oxford nicknames was "Posey"), was an athlete, and so ran with a different set; he was called a "Hearty," as were those Oxford rowers who were members of Corpus Christi crew. Bridges, like Gerard, wrote poetry but never mentioned this to Gerard until after they had both left Oxford, when this avowed commonality opened the door for them to resume and deepen their friendship, primarily through correspondence. Poignantly, the last poem Gerard ever wrote was dedicated to Bridges.

Meanwhile, though, Gerard was closer and in more frequent contact with men like Edward William Urquhart, an older man already graduated from Oxford the year before Gerard entered and now Anglican curate at Saints Philip and James, a High Church parish in the northern part of the medieval city. Urquhart and Gerard appear to have flirted a bit, with each other as with Anglo-Catholicism, and with the tempting possibility of going over to Rome, though Urquhart did eventually marry and never left Anglicanism.[11]

Newman, a former Anglican priest who had "gone over to Rome" in 1845 and who was known then and to posterity as "England's greatest Catholic convert," was the hero of the Anglo-Catholic set of which Gerard became a part. They admired him so much that they intentionally imitated Newman's odd, rather stooped way of walking around campus, and some adopted the long, black, high-buttoned waistcoats that he favored—pejoratively labeled "the Mark of the Beast" by his opponents. Though Newman was no longer at Oxford but had been in Ireland establishing a Roman Catholic university and was now at the Oratory in Birmingham, his memory still stalked the grounds of Oxford. Newman, along with Pusey and John Keble, another English churchman and poet, had begun the Oxford Movement some thirty years before Gerard was to arrive.

Newman was described by his contemporaries as an astonishing orator who could move his listeners to tears with his conviction about Christ; however, his voice, somewhat surprisingly, was described as thin and reedy, his delivery characterized as fairly dispassionate, and his expositions, heavily ratiocinated; this latter, however, worked in his favor, as it provided the Anglo-Catholic set with arguments to use against the Broad Church party. In a series of tracts that earned for him and his circle the name Tractarians, Newman—as well as Keble and Pusey—inveighed against what he called "Bible Religion," or those who worshiped in a nonsacramental way, deriving legalistic syllogisms from Scripture but neglecting the body of Christ. He took aim at powerful, influential contemporary orators such as Liddon whose sermons were wildly popular with Oxford students, asserting that the assent they gave to matters of faith was "notional, not real," and that, like Gerard's father, they reduced church attendance to being a good Englishman, fostering thereby a "national religion," a focus on "living a correct life" and a dilution of Christ's teachings to "sacred scenes and pious sentiments . . . careless of creed and catechism." He excoriated the Broad Church party for allowing "the furniture of their mind" to be a mere "gentleman's knowledge."[12]

Gerard already knew of Newman and of his "turning" (as it was called) to Roman Catholicism because of a family connection through Maria Rosina de Giberne, younger sister of Gerard's favorite uncle, George. Maria may have had an early romance with Newman. An accomplished artist and a woman of deep piety, she became a Tractarian, converted to Catholicism in 1845 under Newman's sway, was presented to Pope Pius, then became a nun, Sister Maria Pia, in 1846. She was thus the first convert to Roman Catholicism in the Hopkins family.[13]

As an undergraduate, Gerard read Newman's *Loss and Gain* and *Apologia pro Vita Sua*, written after Newman quit his post as vicar of St. Mary's, Oxford. Scathingly attacked by Anglican clergyman Charles Kingsley, Newman wrote the *Apologia* to explain his faith. Gerard also read Newman's "Dream of Gerontius" (1865), a poem about a dying man's choices and the path his soul takes to purgatory, where it is not punished but rather purified. Written after Newman's conversion, the poem solidly upheld Roman Catholic doctrine. Gerard was such a devotee of Newman's that the nickname "Gerontius" was given to him by some of his friends. For faith-filled intellectuals, this reading was heady stuff.[14] For Gerard, Newman paved his high road to salvation, a path the very scrupulous, exceedingly conscientious young man increasingly sought. He craved focus, intensity, purity, "that ecstacy / Which to pure souls alone may be" granted.[15] Gerard's perfectionistic personality, prone to extremes, led him to

Newman, who championed a full-hearted dedication to Christ and devotion to Rome.

Newman's influence[16] worked on impressionable Gerard, this rebellious boy paradoxically in search of absolute Authority, and his group of friends, like a magic potion. Gerard literalized the philosophy of Plato and Plotinus he was reading for Greats with Pater, and he applied it now as his template for faith. He was entranced, intoxicated; at last he had found Beauty and Truth. Gerard had found the Cause to which he could consecrate himself: discerning the immanence of divinity.[17] He had found a direction and channeling for his spiritual intensity as well as his artistic impulses. His idols—Newman; Ruskin, whose *Elements of Drawing*, as well as other writings, Gerard was reading; and Pater—all looked upward, in different ways, seeking the higher and perfect forms in which partial beauty here below was fully realized.

Gerard fell in love, perhaps many times and in different ways. In a hero-worshiping way, Gerard adulated and loved Newman. And this love—and, later, others—helped him more fully to love Christ and to know him through a transcendental aesthetics (ultimately, a poetics) that Gerard was to spend his short life developing. This was his vocation: to discern all that was most excellent and lovely in the world and, through that, to elevate himself and others to God. The beauty of Christ, the man-God, was an incarnational beauty he could love without shame or circumspection, with an utter outpouring of all that was best within him.

Yet this was not a culturally easy choice. Gerard at first hid his new faith from his family, knowing that they would be horrified as he increasingly became closer and closer to Roman Catholicism, his beauty-craving soul seeking to saturate itself with holy oil, vestments, incense, chanting, and the daily reception of the host; but, most of all, he sought to satisfy his yearning for Truth.

Another acquaintance, Frederick Gurney, invited Gerard to join the Brotherhood of the Holy Trinity, a student society founded by Pusey, Newman's only associate to remain at Oxford.[18] This was an Anglican lay brotherhood that had a well-deserved reputation for theological conservatism and Roman Catholic inclinations. Gerard never actually joined, but he did attend meetings where he met, and heard the preaching of, Henry Liddon, an Anglo-Catholic faculty sponsor of the Brotherhood, a handsome man and a charismatic personality. As had Newman, Liddon dressed in a cassock and long, woolen black cape (as contrasted with the more businesslike and secular Anglican frock coat) for daily wear, and he made a vow of celibacy, which led many in Gerard's group of friends to profess a similar vow. Liddon also encouraged, as had Newman, frequent confessions and the keeping of a special journal in which to note one's sins.

Some felt that the members of the Brotherhood were degenerate and effete, and this may be why Gerard avoided membership. His hero worship of figures like Newman and Liddon shows that he worshiped a high ethic of personal probity, and Gerard was generally careful to rein in his own wayward impulses. An early play he penned contains this advice, perhaps "to self": "You know what I mean. It is better to conceal at times."[19] The death penalty for sodomy had only been repealed in England very recently, in 1861.[20]

Gerard's personal piety was certainly influenced by some of the Brotherhood's practices. A satire entitled "A Son of Belial" written by fellow student Martin Geldart during the 1860s—such satires were common forms of after-dinner entertainment—again applied to Gerard the sobriquet "Gerontius Manley," a caricature of him as "my ritualistic friend." The scrupulosity of a daily examination of conscience appealed to Gerard's obsessive and perfectionistic personality; though drawn to things he believed he should avoid, he also dreaded sin and strove to avoid contamination. His religious idealism expressed itself in a variety of forms of self-sacrifice. One was particularly difficult for Gerard, with his artistic temperament: he practiced for a full half year, as Pusey had recommended, "the penance of the eyes," an exercise in humility and self-deprivation, determining not to allow himself to raise his gaze from the ground for extended periods of time, sometimes even several months at a stretch, so as not to be tempted by inappropriate forms of beauty.[21] He also, as did members of the Brotherhood, wrapped a flannel chastity band around his lower abdomen, and embraced the practice of fasting for purity.[22] His scrupulosity became stronger, as an entry in his journal dated January 23, 1866, attests, stipulating rules to himself: "For Lent. No pudding on Sundays. No tea except if to keep me awake and then without sugar. Meat only once a day. No verses in Passion Week or on Fridays. No lunch or meat on Fridays. Not to sit in armchair except can work in no other way. Ash Wednesday and Good Friday bread and water."[23] Gerard's excessive scrupulosity of conscience, as the Jesuits would term it, led him to try constantly to self-regulate, to discipline himself, to surpass himself, to be a hero against the world and his desires, to offer these sacrifices for Christ. It was a character trait that would haunt him throughout his life, and one which he would offer, in gratitude for respite from its torments, to "Him Who freed me / From the self that I have been."[24]

These practices may all have been recommended by his Anglo-Catholic mentors[25] and were certainly not unusual for Gerard's time period and the fervid context in which he found himself at Oxford. What does stand out, however, is the intensity—almost emotional desperation—of Gerard's increasingly self-regulated spiritual practices. Fortunately, he was more than bright, for his studies certainly began to cede priority to his religiosity. And the boy who had filled copious artist's notebooks with detailed sketches of the natural world began to fill ledgers with lists of sins and spiritual accountings in a cramped and careful hand.[26] Gerard was a person of vividly imagined, intensely experienced, paradox. It seems almost as though he sought to fit his sensual self into a spiritual straitjacket—one within which, paradoxically, he would be channeled into greater fulfillment.[27] Aesthetics and sanctity would be somehow intertwined in this project. He had yet to work out the details.

He became increasingly convinced of the Real Presence in the Eucharist, believing that reception actually brought the believer into communion with Christ's body and blood and that this was the significance of the sacrifice at the high altar. Anglicanism historically had espoused a variety of beliefs about the significance of Holy Communion, and variations of these are stated in the diverse iterations of the Book of Common Prayer, but none was catechetically mandated, unlike the centrality of the belief for Catholics. A full two years prior to converting to Catholicism, Gerard wrote to a friend, Ernest Coleridge, that "the object of belief is the Real Presence in the Blessed Sacrament." He called religion lacking this belief "somber, dangerous, illogical" and deemed religious observance accompanied by this belief "lovable."[28] Heart had trumped head or, as Newman demonstrated, faith could and did build on reason.

Gerard began regularly to attend St. Thomas, the "highest" of the Anglo-Catholic parishes just off the Oxford grounds. In 1854, its vicar had been one of the first Anglican clergymen in the country since the Reformation of the sixteenth century to resume donning a chasuble, the garment worn during the consecration of the bread and wine. This was a strong sartorial statement of Anglo-Catholic ritual affiliations with Roman Catholicism. This vicar, like many of the so-called Ritualists,[29] held that Newman had brought the Anglo-Catholic wing of the church to a high point and that, after his departure, it was eminently possible and desirable to retain Anglican identity without necessarily following him as converts into the Catholic Church. But although Gerard felt more at home in the hyper-Anglican atmosphere at St. Thomas, he could not agree. At odds with his own father, unable to communicate with him about his theological questions, since his father had adopted a posture of mourning for the dead when he learned of Gerard's plans to convert,[30] Gerard increasingly emulated Newman's example, deliberately adopting him, some have speculated, as a sort of spiritual father figure.

In October 1865, Gerard wrote the poem "The Half-way House," its title deriving from a dismissive comment Newman had made in his *Apologia* characterizing Anglicanism, in his view, as a mere halfway station between atheism and the true church, Catholicism. Clearly Gerard was struggling. He had been reared Anglican, and his father had surely reminded him of the practical component to remaining Anglican, too; he knew that Victorian England rewarded Anglicans, favoring them for governmental positions and high-profile posts. Yet everything in him yearned for the beauty, the certainty, and the ancient tradition of Catholicism. He exclaimed, "My national old Egyptian reed gave way; / I took of vine a cross-barred rod or rood," indicating that "national" religion was not, to him, the true or native one but rather an interloper, "Egyptian," a hybrid or strange form. He chose instead the crucifix. The concluding lines of the poem affirm almost creedally the Real Presence: "enter these walls, one said: / He is with you in the breaking of the bread."[31] Gerard had made his choice. He would enter the Roman Catholic Church and be with his Lord. Lukewarm, "halfway" measures did not suffice for this ardent young man enamored of perfection and absolutes. In his journal for July 17, 1866, Gerard says strongly: "it was this night I believe but possibly the next that I saw clearly the impossibility of staying in the Church of England."[32] He "resolved," however, to make no formal declaration until three months had passed and he had taken his degree. Gerard's belief system was already presenting him with complications, worldly obstructions.

Struggling interiorly with how best to worship, to know himself and to meet his soul's needs, increasingly feeling that to reach clarity on this was a matter of his spiritual salvation, Gerard nonetheless found time for less intense pursuits, vacationing with a chum or two during "Long Vacs" on the Isle of

Wight, where he participated in reading parties and also sketched a good deal, framing his landscapes and seascapes through what he called a "Ruskinesque point of view," and swimming, canoeing, and hiking about country pastures. On these trips, Gerard observed nature with the passionate attentiveness he gave to liturgy. Knowing nature in its most intimate self-revelation through the most minute and exacting process of delineation or depiction gave him a joy, a stabilizing awareness, and elevated consciousness. His prose was painterly, as he strove to incorporate everything he saw, to make it his own. He experienced what he saw in nature in a sensual, indeed multisensorial, way, combining, for example, description of elm trees with comparisons drawn from the human body; the downy sweep of a folded "soft juicy" inner leaf appeared to him to "blaze like an underlip,"[33] how it looks when backlit. His descriptions are so intense, so intricate, that they display the real presence, as it were, of the object on the page. Gerard was developing an incarnational sensibility about poetry, and about the world.

He was also developing a sense of intimacy with nature and devising a technique for unlocking its mysteries, its proximity to its source, its seemingly paradoxical markers of divinity in a material world. Trees were presences to him; stars no mere luminaries but celestial signposts; birds, divine emissaries and figures of God. Natural patterns and movements were signs he could examine and decipher. Waves and water puddles, crystalline sweepings of hoarfrost: these were glyphs of a cosmic code, divine signatures. Gerard's studies of Plato, his interest in things medieval and in Pre-Raphaelite art with its emphasis on the Arthurian legends, all combined to form a somewhat archaic and mystical vision distinct to him. When he described so painstakingly and evocatively what he observed, this was no mere appropriative project; he was seeking intimacy and an opening; he was insinuating himself within another essence. He asserted, "what you look hard at seems to look hard at you," constructing a relationship with objects that magicked them into subjects.[34] He sought to surpass Ruskin by penetrating beneath elaborate surface and detailed rendering to a creative, imaginative, intuitive living-with of the entity he was viewing. This was sacramental; this was incarnational. As God took on humanity in Christ, so Gerard strove to take on complex and rich "otherness," to be both self and it. And his yearning to get below, beneath, beyond whatever confronted him was analogous to his desire to return to the original forms of belief perpetuated in Roman Catholic ritual. His aesthetic sensitivity paralleled, supported, and nourished his religious sensibility.

Although Gerard's explicitly spiritual journals, those in which he recorded thoughts or preoccupations while meditating or praying, for the most part, are no longer extant,[35] those diaries that survive show a jumble of experiences, descriptions, responses, and events, like a vast treasure house from which he was sculpting his own portrait, who he would become in relation to the world. He also used his diaries for quick sketches or for jottings, notations of ideas seized on the fly; one or two lines of verse he would later rework. The journals were young Gerard *in process*. He scribbled in haste and also slowed to carefully inscribe certain thoughts with minute and cramped handwriting; he confided to Robert Bridges that he used a different "hand" for different sorts of thoughts; he meticulously described every angle or facet of what he was observing—a swallow, an oriel window, a ripple on the river. He was making it his own. His comparisons occasionally reflect other preoccupations. For instance, his religious *idée fixe* returns in this description of the sweeps and lines of an alpine snowscape resembling the tucks and folds of an ecclesiastical vestment ("one of [the mountains'] beauties is in nearly vertical places the fine pleatings of the snow running to or from one another, like the newness of lawn in an alb"),[36] the image of a linen ecclesial vestment overlaying natural beauty, underscoring the intimacy between physical world and metaphysical perspective for Gerard. At other times, his metaphors and similes stress the abundant possibilities found solely in the natural world, and they are surprising, original, and unexpected, as when he describes a cloud formation as an exquisitely strutted, buttressed, and molded cathedral: "White-rose cloud formed fast, not in the same density—some caked and swimming in a wan whiteness, the rest soaked with the blue and like the leaf of a flower held against the light and diapered out by the worm or veining of deeper blue between rosette and rosette. Later/ moulding, which brought rain: in perspective it was vaulted in very regular ribs with fretting between."[37] The muscular endeavor of his prose to seize, describe, know, shows a sort of vaunting participation in God's creative act, as though by somewhat brashly acknowledging beauty with his description, Gerard validated what God had done. "His tale and telling," he exulted, "has been given to me."[38] And then Gerard could carry these word pictures away in his journal, back to his bedside, to some safe place, and there exercise an alchemy of the word. More and more, Gerard conceived of the abundant precision of his words as an echo of, an approximation of, a way to reach the Word that had first given all things breath. The young boy who had been master of nature's ceremonies, reader of her mysteries, was now mystic interpreter of God's greater wonders: "*And knew the who and the why; / Wording it how but by him that present and past, / Heaven and earth are word of, worded by.*"[39]

His writing was at the same time an excitement, a joy, and an arduous project. He groped, frustrated at times, for the precise phrase: "brilliancy, sort of starriness: I have not the right word"; "the spraying out of one end I tried to catch but it would have taken hours," he admitted in exhaustion.[40] He seemed to feel a daunting responsibility correctly and fully to describe, at times an almost frantic need to know, a stabbing nostalgia for the essence of these things of the world.

In his journals, too, he took on contemporary idols; he took aim at Matthew Arnold, an extremely popular Victorian poet, for pretentiousness, as well as at Poet Laureate Tennyson for bombastic, insincere formulations. "What have I come across / That here will serve me for comparison? / The sceptic disappointment and the loss / A boy feels when the poet he pores upon / Grows less and less sweet to him, and knows no cause," Gerard bemoaned.[41] He bucked public opinion and dared to criticize some cultural icons. Gerard was developing his own pantheon of heroes and mentors and models—Keats, some Shelley, some Pater and Ruskin and Milton; Shakespeare, of course—but he was also reaching back beyond known figures to an Anglo-Saxon, Old English, primal stew of sounds and rhythms that, when he later went to Wales, boiled over into an intoxicating broth of Celtic music and evocative wordplay. In some of his earliest diary entries at Oxford, he showed the skill and preoccupations of an etymologist; the Hopkins family had loved wordplay, and Gerard excelled at neologisms and the sort of mirror regress of associative sounds: "*Flick, fillip, flip, fleck, flake*," he caroled in an 1863 entry, treating the words as colors in a tone poem: "To *fleck* is the next tone above flick, . . . a piece of light, colour, substance" all connected.[42]

Though himself not yet fully formed, Gerard was already searching for ways to shape his encounter with the world. He went at it with energy, enthusiasm, eccentric dedication. In general, the institutions and figures that peopled his context were not sufficient for him. For the time being, he held himself somewhat aloof, like the Lady of Shalott in Tennyson's poem, brooding, withdrawn, over the small world framed in her distant window. His time had not yet fully come, he felt. "My window shews the travelling clouds, / Leaves spent, new seasons, alter'd sky, / The making and the melting crowds: / The whole world passes; I stand by."[43] This rather vainglorious posture, identifying himself as an alchemist in the city of Oxford, shows the young Gerard wanting either to reach back to an old purity or to leapfrog past the present to some new self-devised sincerity of meaning.

But also there were present-day people to admire, mostly poets, Gerard found. In July of 1864 he was invited to a fete at the home in London of a fellow Balliol student, Frederick Gurney, where Gerard was introduced to the poetess Christina Rossetti. A High Church Anglican with, herself, pronounced sympathies for Roman Catholic liturgy, Rossetti had received critical acclaim for *Goblin Market* and other collections of poems that displayed a spiritually tortured, but ultimately symbolically and theologically reconciled, persona.[44] The shocking sincerity of her verse, its almost audacious oddity and freedom, thrilled Gerard, who wrote of her to his mother that "for pathos and beauty of art, the simple beauty of her work cannot be matched."[45] He also met Swinburne and Keats, both of whom he admired. As already noted, Ruskin had a huge influence on Gerard; Ruskin's *Modern Painters, I–V,* published sequentially in 1843, 1846, 1856, and 1860, defended literary Pre-Raphaelitism as well as the countercultural artistic manifesto of the Pre-Raphaelite Brotherhood, calling for an intensely real approach to nature—a direct rebellion against Sir Joshua Reynolds and classicism—and for beauty coupled with an idealized medievalism. William Michael Rossetti wrote the manifesto, outlining a program of "truth to nature" that included "genuine ideas; [an attentive] study of Nature so as to know how to express them; sympath[y for] what is direct and heartfelt and serious in previous art; [and] the exclusion of what is conventional and self-parading and learned by rote."[46] Gerard's verse, too, would carve new rhythms and sound shapes, blazing a new path for spiritual insight to join with meticulous observations of nature, and rigorously avoiding self-exaltation. Gerard intentionally allied himself with the new generation of artists and writers and artisans who cared deeply about wordsmithing and craftsmanship. For the mid-nineteenth century, this effort was both muscular and metaphysical; to find the right word, turn, evocation, sound, shade, or hue was transformational and required both precision and passion.

In his journals, Gerard seemed almost intoxicated with his efforts and discoveries, these verbal felicitations. But in many ways his life at Oxford had a very prosaic, quotidian side. His studies continued. He excelled in all but theology. He wrote brilliant papers on philosophical questions and scientific matters. He read widely. One attraction was to Savanarola, whose bonfire of the vanities seems to have appealed to Gerard's ascetic side. Like the Florentine figure, Gerard was in love with beauty but afraid at times of the power it could hold over him. Self-deprivation and discipline occasionally presented themselves as ways to protect the self from the world. Yet every time he tried to deny himself, his craving for nature and beauty refused to be repressed. Concerned, perhaps, about his sexuality, which found an echo in his quick and strong response to physical beauty in the world both of nature and of art, he sought to impose a spiritual girdle on the burgeoning world of beauty around him. This was not an idiosyncratic choice; it was advice some Victorian contemporaries also followed.

However, Gerard saw nature as one exceedingly privileged venue for the revelation of God. He was beginning to be bolder, more overt in his very particular profession of faith. And part of this was due to love. When he met Digby Mackworth Dolben in February 1865, Gerard had acknowledged to himself that this encounter was "the single most momentous emotional event" of his life.[47] Somehow, in loving a fellow lover of Christ, however flamboyant and controversial Dolben might have been, Gerard found an increased ability in himself to profess his own love for Christ. And Dolben was all that was beautiful—for Gerard, but also for many others, among them Henry James, who had greatly admired his "classic profile."[48] Although Dolben, like Gerard, came from a resolutely Anglican and anti-Roman family, by 1862 he had embraced ritualism. While still at Eton, he wore the vestments of a tertiary (lay, or unordained) Benedictine, he was caught visiting Jesuits in secret and summarily brought home by his parents so that they could keep a close eye on him, and he wrote floridly religious poetry describing the masculine perfections of the beauty of Christ. Dolben's was a personality that could not be ignored, a presence that flamed brightly. When Dolben visited his distant cousin Bridges in 1865, he and Hopkins seem to have been immediately and strongly drawn to each other and spent most of their time together during his visit. In many ways, they were similar personalities: intense, self-dedicating, scrupulous—both fasting, both practicing forms of penitential discipline—excessive (although Gerard's excesses were more often paradoxical spasms of self-denial), avowed lovers of the Blessed Mother, and teetering "on the edge of the Tiber."

Dolben, a pretty young man with leonine locks and seductive eyes, was a problematic associate. A devotee of Anglo-Catholic ritual, Dolben carried his adoration to extremes, setting up an eccentric form of lay brotherhood, garbing himself as a monk—at a time when the public wearing of Roman Catholic habits was outlawed—and surrounding himself with admiring young men. He intended to become a Roman Catholic priest; he meant, he declaimed, to establish his own order of English Benedictines; and he drew eyes, and intentions, into his orbit. He was gorgeous and poised on the brink of dissolution. Not able to obtain admission to Oxford, he was his father's greatest trial, leading a wayward and seemingly rudderless life, with the exception of his extreme devotion to religiosity. Gerard's letters during his yearlong obsession with him describe Dolben's beauty as "dangerous."[49] Gerard burned many of his personal papers that might have shed further light on their relationship. What is clear is that he felt a great attraction for Dolben, which he also characterized as sinful and confessed to his spiritual director while at Oxford. In June 1865, having met Dolben, Gerard suggestively confided, "He has a sin of mine, he its near brother."[50] And later, Gerard drafted a sort of confession in verse: "Once I turned from thee and hid, / Bound on what thou hadst forbid; / Sow the wind I would; I sinned: /

I repent of what I did."[51] Yet Gerard apprehended God's glory through the beauty he found in the natural world, and Dolben was a resplendent specimen of beauty. In August 1865, Gerard bemusedly permitted himself an awareness of such attraction, admitting, "there's an interest and sweet soul in beauty / Which makes us eye-attentive to the eye / That has it."[52] The natural world—in all its forms, all its creatures, including Dolben—was increasingly for Gerard a privileged theater for the manifestations of God's glory and power.

Gerard and Dolben discussed their faith, wove it into the daily life of the town and gown. Deep in thought, they walked to Seal's Coffee House and down along Oxford canal, passing the Bible stall at St. Giles Fair, perhaps listening to the choristers on the top of Magdalen Tower on May Day or observing parishioners of St. Mary the Virgin "beating the bounds," defining their parish parameters by processing with willow wands on Ascension Day. Still discussing, they dipped in and out of the secondhand bookshops on the High Street and Broad, maybe visiting the Holy Trinity Convent in Woodstock Road. Dolben's penchant for flowing Benedictine robes would have formed an odd mismatch with the Balliol striped tie and jacket Gerard wore, as well as with the dark frock coats and white stocks of the dons. And they may have persuaded each other to make a firmer, formal profession of their Roman Catholic leanings.

Two years before meeting Gerard, Dolben had burned all his poetry, eschewing productions of ambitions and the exaltation of the self. It can be no coincidence that, a scant two years later, before becoming a Jesuit, Gerard would do the same. He had already set himself a precedent; in 1862, Gerard had burned part of his diaries. As one of Gerard's later emulators, T. S. Eliot, was to say: if one really wants to magnify the Word, at a certain point one has to let one's own words lapse into silence.[53] This was to be a defining struggle for Gerard: as his sense of vocation deepened, his urge to write and to create seemed to him suspect, an avenue for "self-parade." And yet, was not the gift God-given? But if God-given, should not its ultimate disposition or survival be decided by God? If all his allegiance and love were to pass through this experience of earthly love, through Dolben, and be directed to the surpassing beauty of Christ, how was he, Gerard, to conceive of his gifts and abilities and urgings? Should there not be a sacrificial holocaust offered to God? Gerard was most assuredly not one of those mid-nineteenth-century dilettantes whom Matthew Arnold decried as "light half-believers of our casual creeds."[54]

Much of this soul-searching began to leak out into Gerard's confessional life and times of private introspection. Dolben, like Gerard, began a more systematic practice of confessional self-disclosure; Gerard's surviving "spiritual diaries" date from this time. He began to keep for his confessor, Liddon, "a little book for sins"; this ledger recorded particular failings through a system of symbols that also noted the penances he was prescribed, or performed on his own, for those sins. Once he had confessed a sin such as, most frequently, masturbation and nocturnal emissions, Gerard drew a line through it with a pencil, but he never entirely erased the notation. It was as though he accepted divine forgiveness but could not quite cease from self-surveillance. He feared his desire; he stared at it, as it were, excessively, out of the corner of his eye. This effort distracted him and tormented him, caused him to distrust himself, stymied him in his creative ventures.

In love, perhaps, with Dolben, as his letters, penned despite the prohibition imposed by his confessor, suggest, Gerard nonetheless relentlessly sought a higher fulfillment than the satisfactions of the flesh, which, son of his era, he had been reared to distrust and despise, anyway. Some years later, in 1877, during his third year of the theologate at St. Beuno's, Gerard visualized his soul as a "caged skylark," a "mounting spirit in his bone-house, mean house." The cage was his rib cage; the lark his heart, pent-up, yet bursting with songs of God's glory. The potential

of the songs was, in itself, salvific, Gerard reassured himself, still
wondering if the actual singing would be problematic, redound-
ing to the glory of the singer, not the Creator. T. S. Eliot was later
to take a similar image and, in "Ash Wednesday," depict dried
bones tumbled about, jumbled about, speaking in the voice of
birds and wondering, like Ezekiel, "shall these bones live?"[55] Gerard's answer to this question came strong and early, affirming the
incarnation paradoxically found in a dung heap, offering hope
through intentional, purificatory self-extrication: "Man's spirit
will be flesh-bound, when found at best, / But úncúmbèred:
meadow-dówn is nót distrèssed / For a ráinbow fóoting it nor hé
for his bónes rísen."[56] Earth is glorified by Christ's resurrection;
marks of Christ's footprints shimmer thereupon; if the focus is
on Christ and not on man, one is "uncumbered, not distressed."
But for now, Gerard's agony was intense. He sought out Liddon
and made a scrupulously detailed confession lasting over an hour
and a half. He loved humanly, yet was prohibited from acting
upon it, indeed self-forbidden to do so. Could this fleshly love
be transformed, provide a "meadow-dówn," a "ráinbow fóoting,"
to Christ?

By March 1866, Gerard had reached a decision. From this spiritual crisis over the interpretation of sensual feelings, Gerard had
finally determined to convert. On November 6, Gerard made an
entry in his journal that opened with a rehearsal of his ongoing
struggle to renounce beauty in whatever form—poetry? art? nature? Dolben?—yet then immediately referred to a letter that
had arrived from Dolben for which Gerard thanked God: "On
this day by God's grace I resolved to give up all beauty until I had
His leave for it; and also Dolben's letter came for which Glory
to God."[57] Dolben's letter is not extant. Was Gerard grateful that
Dolben had somehow released him from his relationship? Or
did he take the arrival of the letter as a sign of divine permission
to continue it? The complexity of Gerard's feelings for Dolben
has been much scrutinized by scholars.[58] What is clear, however,

is the lack of clarity Gerard himself felt. To extricate himself from this emotional morass, he decided for Christ, not Dolben. Or for Christ through Dolben. Unlike his contemporary Walt Whitman (to whom—much to his genuine disgust—Gerard's verse was later likened),[59] Gerard refused to allow the desires of the flesh to prevail as normative or determinative; they must be transmuted, directed like icons toward the divine. Gerard's diary shows him horrified by sexual attraction to the suffering, crucified Christ.[60] Utter dedication to God must be his only safe way. Gerard's doubts about the Church of England's efficacy in obtaining salvation had become more than occasional worries; the issue was now crucial, a matter of his immortal soul. He would convert to Roman Catholicism, the traditional, steady repository of both papal infallibility and the apostolic succession. On Christmas Day 1866, Gerard wrote joyfully, the decision now taken, of "the sight of Him Who freed me / From the self that I have been," and urged, "Now begin, on Christmas day."[61]

And yet this joy was not untrammeled. Back at home, he had a Christmas Day discussion with his mother concerning the communion of saints that left her in tears, her concern not so much, as was Gerard's, with the state of his soul but rather, quite seriously and pragmatically, with the state of his present prospects since, in Victorian England, a conversion from Anglicanism to Catholicism cut one loose from all social standing, all possibilities of material and professional advancement. Her son would become a pariah, as he himself attested, figuring himself as a swallow, with "all-accepting fixèd eye," scoping out the vastness of sky yet having no "permanence in the solid world."[62]

Gerard was confronted with strenuous parental opposition. He also faced ostracism by his peers. Further, he risked losing his Oxford credentials in his final year, since his conversion to Roman Catholicism would hinder nearly all academic and professional opportunities, barring one from fellowships and tutorials, as well as making it impossible in good conscience to attend Anglican chapel, which was compulsory in order to matriculate. He did receive some support and encouragement in his decision from an itinerant Roman Catholic priest named T. J. Capel, who often visited Oxford to, as the Anglican clergy pejoratively termed it, "make raids" on undergraduates. During a friendly ramble with a fellow undergraduate named Addis, a lapsed Anglican with whom Gerard had begun to share rooms out of college while working through his decision to convert, Gerard and Addis had shared doubts about the authenticity of Anglicanism, and he had also earlier had a conversation (perhaps the first Gerard had ever had with a Catholic cleric) with the Benedictine Dom Paul Raynal at the Cathedral Priory of St. Michael, in which they discussed the doubtful validity of Anglican orders.[63] Gerard continued to bolster himself in his decision by making friends with other undergraduates who were contemplating conversion to Catholicism.

But most important in Gerard's decision and perseverance in it was Newman. On August 28, 1866, inspired by Newman's reputation and tales of his avuncular kindness toward undergraduates as well as the great decision the great man himself had made to leave the Church of England and "go over to Rome," Gerard wrote, not without trepidation, asking Newman for help, guidance, and information. Newman had been away on holiday, traveling through Switzerland, and did not return home to the Birmingham Oratory until September 7. Confronted with a daunting pile of unanswered mail, Newman nonetheless sorted through it and must have performed some sort of spiritual triage, for he responded to Gerard by September 14. Newman reassured him and offered to meet with him. In Gerard's letter, Gerard both professed his desire to be received into the Catholic Church and also underscored that this was not a measure he conceived of as comfortable or something over which he could in any way compromise: he wanted to exercise a most rigorous and fulsome faith, with no "minimizing Catholicism" acceptable to him, and in order to do that, he needed clarity on "certain formally open points."[64] The phrases crackle with Gerard's intensity and excitement, his determination to stay this course but also to know fully where he was venturing. Gerard was craving certainty that the theology he espoused, and the piety he would embrace for the rest of his life, were fully comprehensible to him as well as demonstrably correct. He was not rushing blindly in; he was schooling himself, in an ascetic way with all deliberation and preparation for the stripping away of former things, for a fully chosen life.

Gerard planned carefully for the visit. On September 1, just after returning from a family vacation on the Isle of Wight, during which Gerard's brother Arthur had coaxed the truth out of him regarding his plans for conversion, Gerard went to visit Bridges, who lived not far from the Birmingham Oratory. By September 22, Newman and Gerard had met at the Birmingham Oratory, an imposing structure in the style of the Italian Renaissance, sure to appeal to Gerard's senses, with its quiet pink stone cloister, just off the main road, and ornate high altar, certain to soothe his spirit.

Newman had founded the Oratory in 1849, after traveling to Rome and obtaining permission from Pope Pius IX to live within an English Catholic community similar to that established by the sixteenth-century saint Philip Neri. Saint Neri was convinced that music elicited noble emotions in men and had structured his common life around the performances of sacred music, in an "oratory." Seeking to do the same, Newman called his building an oratory, a space for prayer and music. Newman himself played a small violin and continued to do so regularly in worship services. He gathered about him a small band of like-minded believers, among them Frederick William Faber, a fellow convert from the Oxford Movement, and they took vows. Initially they resided at St. Anne's Church on Alchester Street. They briefly held services in a converted gin distillery. They then purchased land and relocated, broke ground in 1850, and the church, dedicated to the Immaculate Conception, was completed two years later, quickly becoming a parish center ministering to all of Birmingham's Catholics. A scant ten years later, Newman founded the Oratory School there as a Catholic alternative to Eton. Newman lived on-site in Oratory House from 1852 until 1890, except for the four years he spent in Ireland.[65]

Within the resonant walls of the Oratory, the tall, gangly, quiet older cleric bent to hear the agitated confessions and impassioned queries of the intense, nervous, diminutive young man with the piercing eyes. They had so much in common: a passionate love for music; a deep dedication to the Blessed Mother; the yearning to find truth and tradition in Roman Catholicism; even Newman's sojourn in Ireland was eventually to be retraced by Gerard. Gerard may have felt as though he were divinely ordained to follow in Newman's footsteps. A few days after the visit, an admiring Gerard wrote a chatty letter, sounding much relieved, to a somewhat uncomprehending Bridges, telling him how approachable and amiable and even witty Newman had been. More importantly, Newman had been Socratic, leading Gerard to elaborate on his own profession of faith, encouraging him to examine his reasons. Newman was also gracious toward the Tractarians at Oxford; when Gerard protested at their blindness, Newman allowed as how brilliant men—perhaps even more so than those less intelligent—can become ensnared by their infatuation with their own intellect and reason, producing what Newman characterized as "invincible ignorance" and which Gerard promptly summed up as a "bird's eye view of Oxford." Without directly telling Gerard what to do—for it was a dangerous course indeed upon which he was embarked, Newman knew that well; and yet, it was the salvation of his soul that was concerned—"he asked questions which made it clear for me how to act," and "when I had given my arguments and said I cd. see no way out of them, he laughed and said 'Nor can I.'"[66]

Prior to their meeting, still questioning whether Anglican sacraments and holy orders were valid, Gerard had been continuing to make his confession to an Anglican priest but was attending Roman Catholic Mass at the mission chapel of St. Ignatius at Oxford, across the Magdalen Bridge. This sort of spiritual mugwumpery now became intolerable to Gerard, and he began exclusively to worship as a Catholic.

Newman and Gerard had agreed that Gerard would return to the Oratory in October at the beginning of the new term in order to be received into the Roman Catholic Church. He would be "received," as he was already Anglican; had he been a nonconformist, he would have been required to convert. Gerard had thought to make a Christmas retreat at the Oratory prior to taking the final step, but on October 15 he was so distressed by his parents' opposition to his plans, as well as resistant to their demand that he at least temporize until he had finished his degree, that he wrote to Newman asking for a meeting on October 21. Newman acquiesced, and on this date received Gerard into the Roman Catholic Church. This was not a full change; confirmation was deferred. Newman then advised Gerard to forgo the Christmas retreat in favor of fulfilling his "first duty." Gerard must return to his family and take the time to mull over his confirmation, which Archbishop Henry Edward Manning later administered on November 4, 1866. Gerard's roommate Addis was also confirmed.

At every turn, when Newman had so many opportunities to solidify Gerard's decision, he instead sagely temporized, deftly muting Gerard's ardent, youthful, and characteristic enthusiasm to ensure that the final decision taken would be sincere and heartfelt, an enduring call and permanent alteration of life. He further guided Gerard in his choice of order, recognizing that the attraction Gerard felt to the Benedictines would not be as helpful for Gerard's temperament as would the more soldierly discipline of the Society of Jesus: "the Jesuits . . . will bring you to heaven," he assured Gerard.[67]

Although he could not know this, Gerard's life was to slice itself neatly into two halves. At the time he became a Roman Catholic, he had already lived a near-exact half of his life as an Anglican.

CHAPTER 2   DEDICATION

Hope holds to Christ the mind's own mirror out
To take His lovely likeness more and more.
It will not well, so she would bring about
A growing burnish brighter than before. [1]

AGAINST ALL ODDS, and due to the good will of a few of his tutors, Gerard completed his Greats examinations in June 1867. But this same very emotional and portentous year of 1867, on August 30 Gerard received a letter from his school friend V. S. Coles conveying the shattering news that Digby Dolben had died on June 28, aged only nineteen. He had drowned in the River Welland while swimming with a ten-year-old boy; Dolben had possibly suffered a cerebral hemorrhage. Although Dolben and Gerard had only had the one brief encounter, Gerard's personality and piety had both been deeply marked by it. The draft of his response to Bridges's letter survives; at the top of the first page, in Gerard's hand, are the words "tristi tu, memini" ("you were sad, maiden").

Sometime earlier, back in Hampstead, on May 11, probably in imitation of Dolben's own previous bonfire and certainly as an offering to him, but also as a dedicatory holocaust to God, Gerard had taken the step that has baffled and horrified later generations of poets and scholars: he burned most of his extant poetry. [2] Perhaps Gerard did not recall that several of his friends, among them Bridges, possessed many of the poems in original manuscript form. And, actually, Gerard was fairly casual about variants and manuscript fragments of his poems anyway, confiding much later to Bridges, who had pasted those that Gerard had sent to him into a bound volume for his personal use, that he found the process of rewriting and constructing a "fair copy" "repulsive, and let [the poems] lie months and years in rough copy."[3] In any event, the gesture of extreme self-censorship was sincere and intransigent, deemed a "slaughter of the innocents," as though he were killing his spiritual progeny.

Despite his grief over the death of Dolben and his own self-questioning, Gerard persevered in his studies and was permitted to graduate from Oxford with a first-class degree a year later. Soon after, he made the retreat at the Birmingham Oratory as he had earlier intended. He took lodgings with a serious-minded side-whiskered fellow convert named Alfred William Garrett, who had also stood up in church for him as his godfather and sponsor. They found rooms near the Roman Catholic church of St. Clement's in Holywell. This small town in Cambridgeshire was renowned for its holy well from which water from the nearby River Ouse could be drawn. A church had stood on the site continuously from at least AD 990, and St. Clement's itself dated from the fourteenth century, with a sixteenth-century tower added later. Garrett and Gerard gathered with others at the famed Ye Old Ferry Boat Inn and ruminated over the young woman reputed to have killed herself at the holy well, Juliet, whose ghost could sometimes be seen on St. Patrick's Eve. Gerard's natural propensity for fairy stories and supernatural phenomena, especially miraculous occurrences, was stirred. His inclination to imbue nature and physical occurrences with a spiritual significance became more pronounced as his devotion to the Roman Catholic Church, with its panoply of saints and martyrs, and its acceptance of miracles, deepened.

Newman suggested to Gerard that he continue to feel his way forward in his vocation by taking on some teaching of Catholic youth, but at the time Gerard was quite sure that he did not want to teach. After Dolben's death, Gerard continued to question his

own motivations and aspirations, and to doubt his own achieve-
ments. The former Gerard must also die; to serve God fully, Gerard believed, he must expunge from himself all worldly ambition
and, yes, lust. Gerard was cutting himself off radically from his
former way of life, though this could be a struggle: Gerard confided, "Part I like and part I hate the fall."[4]

Henceforth, he would be wholly consecrated to God. Three
days later, May 5, 1868, he carefully inscribed in his journal: "resolved to be a religious."[5] His journals show a preoccupation with
renunciation and self-restraint, an anxiety about his self-control,
and an urge toward self-immolation twinned with a hint of what
would become a pattern of oscillation between highly febrile,
emotionally charged, and spiritually intense states and periods of
dullness and apathy, even despair. "I once wanted to be a painter,"
the young man confided, as though his life were already spent.
"But even if I could I would not now I think, for the fact is that
the higher and more attractive parts of the art put a strain upon
the passions which I should think it unsafe to encounter. I want
to write still and as a priest I very likely can do that too, not
so freely as I should have liked, e.g. nothing or very little in the
verse way, but no doubt what would best serve the cause of my
religion."[6] He was intentionally tightening a spiritual straitjacket
around himself.

And yet, he did continue to write, although he did not seek to
publish. A scant year after Dolben's death, Gerard's poem "The
Elopement" appeared in the Oratory magazine the *Early Bird*.[7]
In it, Gerard described the entrancement of a lover yearning after
another. Gerard flung the lover forward; he fairly flogged the
verses onward: "O heart, have done, you beat you beat so high."
Nature conspired in his feeling of pressure and haste: "The stars
are packed so thick to-night / They seem to press and droop and
stare, / And gather in like hurdles bright / The liberties of air," but
nature also revealed that the longed-for joining together would
not transpire: "the little hurling sound / To the point of silence in

the air / Dies off in hyacinthed ground, / And I should find him there." The poem ended in tragic loss, the lover buried in "the plot I find my true love by."[8] The hyacinths are obliquely revealing: in Greek mythology, Hopkins's scholarly forte, Hyacinthus was a lovely young man struck down prematurely by the gods, and the flower evokes youthful magnificence and beauty as well as funerals and death. Appearing in a school organ for young men, not in printed but only in handwritten form, the poem aptly laid a literary wreath at Dolben's feet.

Gerard had finally decided to accept Newman's invitation to teach as a fifth-form junior master at the Edgbaston Oratory School in Birmingham. A fifth-form master would get to know his students well by teaching as a generalist, instructing in both classical and modern subjects. Even given his newfound zeal and clarity of purpose, in these circumstances Gerard was still despondent. His friendship with one of the other masters, Henry Challis, who had been a High Church friend of Gerard's at Oxford and had converted a bit before him, offered some comfort. And the distractions of teaching fifth form, with students aged fifteen and sixteen, may have helped somewhat; he was very busy, taking on the tutoring of precocious private pupils on weeknights. He called these latter his "spiritual children." The curriculum laid considerable stress on history and the classics, and mastery of the material was crucial if the Oratory, founded, as Newman phrased it, both "to Anglicize Catholicism and vice versa,"[9] was to compete with schools like Eton. In 1855, the first civil service exam had been imposed, and more and more, students were required to demonstrate their proficiency in this formatted manner rather than in the more informal, question-and-answer interview approach on which secondary schools and institutions of higher learning had formerly relied. In addition to the teaching and individualized tutorials, the life at the Oratory asked more of its faculty. Newman played violin in the school chamber music group, and Gerard, ever assiduous to emulate his spiritual father, began

himself to take violin lessons. He was overworked and emotionally exhausted, and he confided in his correspondence, in what
amounts to an eerily prophetic leitmotif for the remainder of his
existence: "teaching is very burdensome. I have not much time
and almost no energy to do anything on my own account. One
sees and hears nothing and nobody here."[10]

Gerard was caught up in teaching, yet all the while he pondered the calling of priest. He scrutinized this change of state,
in his characteristically anxious way, from every angle. "If I am
a priest it will cause my mother great grief and this preys on my
mind," he confided to his journal.[11] In an effort to stop dithering,
he left the Oratory after hearing the preaching of Father Henry
Coleridge, SJ, himself a convert, and went to Manresa House, the
Jesuit formation umbilicus, to make a retreat at Easter, March
1868, to decide whether or not he would be ordained.

But first, almost a decision in itself, as he hesitated between
becoming a Benedictine, as Dolben had thought to do, and joining the Society of Jesus, as Newman advised, Gerard decided to
take a trip through Switzerland, the country most recently to
have barred Jesuits from practicing within its borders. Although
Switzerland allowed the practice of both Catholicism and Prot-
estantism, article 51 of the Swiss constitution explicitly prohibited Jesuits from exercising pedagogical or clerical functions in
the state because of their perceived ultramontane traditionalism,
which was seen as a threat to national equilibrium. Gerard was
clearly leaning toward becoming a Jesuit, and he wanted to visit
Switzerland, where he had never before traveled, before cutting
himself off from this opportunity. As before, when he had burned
his poetry, Gerard was now taking steps to shut doors on himself, clustering his world into a close cloister of preoccupation
with Christ.

The Society of Jesus appealed to Gerard for many reasons,
not least its controversial reputation for intransigence and arch-
fidelity to the pope. The Jesuits seemed to him the most Catholic

of the Catholics; styled "soldiers for Christ" by their founder Ignatius of Loyola, the Jesuits required a longer period of formation
than other orders and, in fact, were not an order but rather a society—meaning they had no set "motherhouse." For that reason,
they were itinerants, sent out where needed, under obedience,
like an army obeying military orders. Gerard's high ideal of beautiful manhood serving Christ in chivalric fashion drew him to
the Society of Jesus. This may have seemed an odd choice for the
frail Gerard of contemplative temperament, as Jesuits were men
of action. He was seeking to shape himself to be other than he
was, asking the supreme sacrifice of himself all along the line to
attest to his great love for Christ.

On May 20, before leaving for Switzerland, he wrote to Father Alfred Weld, requesting permission to apply to join the Society. Father Weld was provincial of the English Province, having
been appointed in 1864. Quite young for a Jesuit administrator
of such caliber, aged forty-one, Father Weld had been professor
of science at Stonyhurst as well as editor at Manresa of the pri-
vately printed and circulated in-house publication called *Letters
and Notices*, which detailed events of exclusively religious interest to the Society.[12] Gerard also wrote to Newman, definitively
informing him of his decision, dating from May 14, 1868, to
become a Jesuit.[13]

Briefly back in Oxford for a reunion with friends, Gerard
visited with Swinburne on Degree Day, capered and consorted
with the bohemian circle of Oxford associates that still attracted
him, scrawled several boyishly lighthearted entries in his journal,
then headed for Switzerland in the company of his friend Edward
Bond. Capped with a round-brimmed straw hat, clad in a tweed
jacket and stout shoes, wielding a walking stick, Gerard and Bond
rambled, as they had formerly wandered in the Lake District, pic-
nicked and lounged about in upland Swiss meadows, gathering
great bunches of cerulean blue harebells and bedecking the brims
of their hats with them, "lunching by a waterfall."[14] Gerard was

happy to have companionship but quickly found a need for time and space to be solitary, observing, as he would for the rest of his life, that "even with one companion ecstasy is almost banished: You want to be alone and to feel that, and leisure—all pressure taken off."[15] The landscape of Switzerland, mountainous and rugged, with innumerable waterfalls and towering pines, must have been a revelation to Gerard spiritually as well as a challenge physically, requiring strenuous mountaineering. He was often breathless, nearly overmatched. Gerard's response to the massiveness of the landscape was to focus on details, to micro-process it.

Unlike Wordsworth and Coleridge,[16] rapt in contemplation of sublime vastness, Gerard "spiritualized the ordinary" and "spiritualized from below,"[17] finding the mountainous grandeur more knowable in its discrete particularities, such as the patterns formed by layers of snow, for instance. He had never before seen the like of this demanding landscape, and the confrontation with a soaring panorama seems to have inspired him and called to his sense of duty. Switzerland also prompted Gerard to resort to his customary approach to nature, a near microscopic concentration on often quixotic aspects,[18] or details others would overlook, applying a sort of textual pressurizing of the detail to explore it fully. He began to "read" nature, scrutinizing it for its iconic meaning, which would point it beyond itself.[19] Craving the intensity of sensation that he experienced both in nature and in his spiritual states, Gerard increasingly withdrew into himself over the month's duration of the journey.

The exquisitely detailed observations in his travel journal took time to record and also provided him with time alone. And he began to reflect on, and even to theorize about, the effect nature had on him, in a very directed and complex way, developing an idiosyncratic vocabulary that he applied to various natural phenomena. The terminology he arrived at would be further deepened and nuanced a few years later, when he made the serendipitous discovery of the medieval theologian Duns Scotus and Scotus's concept of *haeccitas*, or the unique and particular "thingness" of each individual thing in the world. For now, Gerard began to develop his ideas of what he called "inscape" and "instress," theoretical categories he had first mentioned in notes for a brilliant undergraduate paper he wrote for Pater on Parmenides. In another essay, "On Personality, Grace and Free Will," Gerard elaborated on these ideas, ruminating over the way in which different selves or different personalities in nature are then "clothed or overlaid with a nature." Once so "clothed or overlaid," the natural thing becomes, for Gerard, an "inscape," with its own essence peculiar to itself alone; the natural thing does not blend into other natural things or blur together, but rather upholds its distinctiveness, Gerard maintained, "according to the will of the Creator."[20] And he exclaimed ecstatically, in this vein, "How fond of and warped to the mountains it would be easy to become! For every cliff and limb and edge and jutty [*sic*] has its own nobility."[21]

The young man who had noted in his journal of sins a certain horrified fascination with cruelty to insects[22] was now atoning for that youthful disregard of all of God's creatures. Nature was rapidly becoming for him the privileged zone for awareness of the divine, in large measure because of the intricate detail and difference of all creatures. He saw through a spiritual lens; while Darwin sought evidence of evolution and change, Gerard noted documentation of specialness, sameness, absolute identity in inscape and its effect on him: his response, generated by the inscape of the thing, he called "instress." The term was almost musical, like a downbeat or rhythm or rest; the various and multifaceted forms of natural life clustered like notes on a ruled page of musical composition. He saw it, and he heard it. It was for him a great symphony composed of particularities, and so would his poetry become. For now, there were hints and foreshadowings in his prose.

The trip to Switzerland proved a laboratory for his later poetic experimentation with meter, accent, and stress and the invention of new words to express his intense, ecstatic encounter with nature as a revelation of the divine. Contemplating a mountain slope near Meyringen, Switzerland, Gerard observed how each of the sycamore trees growing along the slope had been affected by the pattern of wind and precipitation in a different way, their shapes twisting and shifting to accommodate the pressure of natural forces. These sycamores were, for him, individual personalities, and he wrote of them as "scantily leaved, sharply quained and accidented by perhaps the valley winds, and often most gracefully inscaped."[23] Using "accidented," a neologism derived from both Old French and Middle English evoking irregularities of surface, and "quained," a term from Middle English conveying sorrow, Gerard succeeded in subtly suggesting a personality of melancholy, perhaps submission to the elements, a gracious acceptance by a population of individuals who suffered and endured, to the trees on the slope. This most likely unconscious strategy of evoking personality from the individual shapes and stuff of nature was soon to become more intentional and developed in Gerard's poetry, and his evocative prose descriptions would often be reprised, incorporated directly into his verse.

On August 30, Gerard seems to have experienced a sort of epiphany; his prose flames with the fire of personal, embodied experience as, again describing trees, this time ash trees, he wrote, "Putting my hand up against the sky whilst we lay on the grass I saw more richness and beauty in the blue than I had known of before." He situated himself within this shimmering, changed nature, a world so alight with the grandeur of God that shone forth so brightly that it illuminated the interstices between his fingers as though they were so many miniature stained glass windows: "It was not transparent and sapphire-like but turquoise-like, swarming and blushing round the edge of the hand and in the pieces clipped in by the fingers, the flesh being sometimes sunlit, sometimes glassy with reflected light, sometimes lightly shadowed in that violet one makes with cobalt and Indian red," he marveled.[24]

The description possesses elements of an out-of-body experience in that Gerard ceased to speak of himself as himself. He no longer recognized his fingers as his own but referred to them as if they were a phenomenon separate from him, speaking of "the fingers" and "the hand" and "the flesh." The experience enraptured him and led to a suspended time of self-forgetting. And yet, he was still himself—simply in abeyance; he still expressed the typical aspects of his own "Gerardness," evoking painterly chiaroscuro and a palette of vivid colors characteristic of his artistic interests. This state of spiritual capaciousness—of being both self and other—is the very definition of mystic experience.[25] And, increasingly, this would become Gerard's preferred mode of being.

Ten years later, in October 1878, Gerard wrote "Rosa Mystica," whose rhythm, language, and preoccupations recall, in tenor if not actual content, this altered state on the mountaintop in Switzerland: "The rose in a mystery, where is it found? / Is it anything true? Does it grow upon ground?— / It was made of earth's mould but it went from men's eyes / And its place is a secret and shut in the skies."[26] That which is natural yields its deepest essence to that which is divine; its ordinariness becomes tinged with, transmuted by, mystery. The gaps between Gerard's fingers, splayed against the light, became apertures through which he beheld God's glory.

So striking and imbued with significance was this epiphanic experience in the meadow for Gerard that he later explicitly invoked it, only slightly altering the prose journal version to incorporate it into his 1883 poem entitled "The Blessed Virgin Compared to the Air We Breathe," in which he wove a web of words to show that Mary herself is "[our] atmosphere" that wraps us round: "I say that we are wound / With mercy round and round / As if with air: the same / Is Mary, more by name." Condensing his epiphanic experience to its two catalysts, air and light, then interposing the substance of the flesh to be transformed, Gerard enjoined his reader, "Nay do but stand / Where you can lift your hand / Skywards: rich, rich it laps / Round the four fingergaps. / Yet such a sapphire-shot, / Chargèd, steepèd sky will not / Stain light."[27] Gerard's intensely private, personal experience of revelation[28] now became something he sought to share through his poetry with others, offering a technique, a way to produce a similar illumination. All mystical experiences possess an element of mediated presence.[29] Here, Gerard's verses are the intermediary, as Mary is the intercessor before her Son, and as Christ is the cosmic mediator.

Having determined to become a priest, Gerard now began to envision himself functioning in that role, imbuing his verses with power to provoke spiritual transformation. His phrasing took on an incantatory cadence.[30] He did not describe his own fingers here; he did not, as he had formerly, use neuter pronouns but rather recommended that the reader appropriate a similar experience for himself ("you can lift your hand"). The experience is one of willing self-insertion into the divine, so that "rich, rich," it will overlap. And it is an experience of transcendent, all-surpassing perfection, as attested to by the repetition of the perfect number seven further along: "Blue be it: this blue heaven / The seven or seven times seven / Hued sunbeam will transmit / Perfect, not alter it."[31]

Switzerland was the beginning of a divine, poetic initiation akin to the celebrated epiphany another wordsmith and experimenter, James Joyce, was to experience on the seashore in *Portrait of the Artist as a Young Man*. The Swiss mountains, alien to what he had formerly known, somehow provided an impetus for Gerard's conjoined artistic and spiritual breakthrough: "And its place is a secret and shut in the skies." Gerard, poised on the brink of accepting his vocation, remembered his childhood self, the small mystical initiate. Master of mysteries, he now interpreted what he saw and experienced in a theological framework. Just so, therefore, the mystical rose, in all its sanguinary beauty, for

Gerard could only symbolize Christ, bleeding red for the world. "Is Mary the rose then? Mary the tree? / But the blossom, the blossom there, who can it be?— / Who can her rose be? It could be but one: / Christ Jesus our Lord, her God and her son . . . / When the rose ran in crimsonings down the cross-wood!"[32] In Switzerland, Gerard began very fully to marry his yearning for God with his passion for natural beauty.

He also was brought up short by the paltry presence of Catholics there, commenting in his journal that it was difficult, very distressing to him, not to be able to meet his weekly obligation of attending Mass. On July 19 he wrote, "Sunday, but no Catholics, I found, at Meyringen," and again, a week later, he found small consolation: "There was no church . . . but there was to be mass said in the little chapel for the guides going up [the mountain face] at two o'clock in the morning and so I got up for this, my [sun]burnt face in a dreadful state. . . . It was an odd scene: two of the guides or porters served; the noise of a torrent outside accompanied the priest."[33] He yearned for the Catholic parishes that he had visited at home and at Oxford and during nearby countryside rambles, even seeking to discern in natural forms of the Swiss landscape the shapes of churches: "In coming down the Faulhorn saw the Finster Aarhorn at last, lonely, standing like a high-gabled steeple."[34] Was it the Finster, or Gerard, who was "lonely"? It was time to return home.

The time had come for Gerard to dedicate himself intentionally. He could no longer tolerate the ambiguity in which he had abided. Back home in England, near Hyde Park, at Roehampton—renamed Manresa by the Jesuits in memory of the rock and cave where Ignatius had experienced the spiritual illuminations that led to his *Spiritual Exercises*—Gerard requested ordination as a member of the Society of Jesus.

He was young, only twenty-four, when the customary age for a Jesuit to be fully through formation was thirty-three, recalling the age at which Christ had finished his earthly ministry, and Gerard was eager and ardent and very naïve. He was also physi-

cally frail and, as became increasingly evident, emotionally fragile. But he was entirely convinced of the rightness, the necessity,
the beauty of what he had decided to do, and saw his choice as
the hidden, secret fruit, the culmination of a decision taken long
before he had ever himself become aware of it, and this, above all,
would sustain him: "The silent conviction that I was to become
a Catholic has been present to me" for quite some time, and was
revealed to him on "a day of the great mercy of God." His choice
was foreordained, and he had now only to live into it, to inhabit
it fully.[35]

At Roehampton, a primarily Georgian village in southwest
London reached by Putney Bridge, he found another Hopkins,
a fellow novice. Nicknamed the "gentle Hop," Gerard enjoyed
the company of Frederick, called "the genteel Hop." The Jesuit
novices lived in austere, unheated, curtained cubicles sparsely
furnished with a small desk, a chamber pot, and a washbasin.[36]
There was no door, so that secret sins could not be cultivated, and
surveillance of the novices was customary. "Special friendship"—
male-to-male intimacy—was especially frowned upon.

Early on in the novitiate, they all made a Long Retreat.[37] This
entailed an entire month of silence; no correspondence or contact with the outside world was permitted, either. Reading was allowed but only, as had been the case for Ignatius of Loyola during
his convalescence from a leg injury, the lives of the saints—none
of the literature, philosophy, or mythology that had nourished
Gerard's poetic soul. The retreat house, although a rather ele-
gant, warm, fawn-hued stone from the outside, lacked attractive
interior appointments; it was intentionally stark and isolating.
Art—painting, sculpture, decorative moldings—was viewed as
an irrelevant distraction.

Novices had to learn to subordinate their will to that of their
superiors, performing any task requested of them without question, be it emptying a slop bucket or digging up the turnip bed.
The Long Retreat was the beginning of consecration, of death

to the former self and its attachments. To that end, use of the "discipline," a penitential whip of leather or knotted rope, was advised; some had chains or studs that dug into unruly flesh. Further, bathing was permitted only once during the retreat; the remainder of the time, the novices were allowed to apply "modesty powder" to neutralize body odors.

Designed to be transformative, the Long Retreat was also deeply traumatic for many. Several had emotional breakdowns, and the health of some novices suffered. Bridges was later to opine that the untimely death of his friend was due in large part to the austerities imposed on Gerard at this time.[38] Nonetheless, those who persevered were given Jesuit garb at the end of the exacting thirty days; Gerard recorded receiving old, used garments, a hand-me-down knee-length gown, and darned stockings.

Clothed like fully formed Jesuits, the novices would henceforth have their days regulated by bells. Entering chapel, the novices stood until the examen bell was rung. A novice designated the "beadle" was responsible for maintaining a log of activities as well as for scheduling the services the novices provided to local parishes. Not all was austerity; at times the novices were given beer for supper, but the time allotted for its consumption was strictly regulated. Everything was scheduled, slots of time tightly synchronized as at a military encampment.

During the two-year novitiate, they learned to compose and deliver sermons. They were also permitted some distraction; they mounted theatrical productions with religious themes and took turns listening to and critiquing each other's sermons. Gerard came in for a considerable amount of joshing because of his tendency to enter into extensive and unnecessary detail when trying to convey a biblical anecdote. But he was popular, as he had been at Oxford, on the whole; his eccentricities, however, were beginning to become more pronounced and came in for some comment. One novice described finding Gerard fascinated, peering intently at the iced-over sprayings of urine from early morning trips to the outdoor privy; he was discerning a pattern and a structure of beauty in them, he said, a bit oddly. And he wore ladies' slippers to warm his tiny feet. This, too, elicited some teasing.[39]

For the most part, gone were the frolicsome days of leisure and punting along the river that Gerard had so enjoyed as an undergraduate, although there were periods for rest allotted also, and it was a welcome refreshment to walk and read in the garden while strolling with other novices. After his first year, Gerard became the beadle and showed an organizational ability commensurate with his scrupulous and meticulous nature. That same year, 1869, the Jesuits established St. Joseph's Church in Roehampton in order to better supply the needs of the outlying area, and Gerard and his fellow novices also served there.

The trials and discipline of the Long Retreat and the formative process of the novitiate were not only educational in purpose. They were also intended to shape young Jesuits ready to serve the Society in any capacity, to go wherever sent at a moment's notice, and to practice obedience in all circumstances. And the cultural context of Victorian England was hardly well disposed to Jesuits. A fledgling Jesuit would have to assume that his evangelization and proselytizing outside of any but the most faithful Catholic circles would be suspect.

Hostility in England to Roman Catholicism was longstanding. During the Reformation, a recusant, someone who refused to join, or objected to, the Church of England and who was loyal to the Roman Catholic Church, was perceived as a traitor to England. In 1593, severe penalties, among them fines, confiscation of all personal property, imprisonment, and even death, were imposed against "Popish recusants." Although the Recusancy Acts promulgated under Elizabeth I were repealed in 1650, penalties continued to be imposed against recusants, and restrictions against the practice of Roman Catholicism remained in effect until the Catholic Emancipation Act of 1829. In

1851, Parliament put into effect the Ecclesiastical Titles Act, an anti–Roman Catholic piece of legislation that made it a criminal offense for anyone outside the Church of England to use an episcopal title in the United Kingdom, thereby rendering it impossible for a Roman Catholic hierarchy to organize under overseeing bishops. This act was a response to a series of "no popery" riots in major cities such as Liverpool in 1850. Anti-Catholic factions of the government, including then prime minister John Russell, incited popular uprisings in response to the Catholic Church under Pope Pius IX setting up its own network of Roman Catholic bishops in England. Over 900,000 British Protestants signed a petition, submitted to the Crown, denouncing the action of the Catholic Church as "papal aggression."[40]

The Tractarian Movement, begun at Oxford, and so also called the Oxford Movement, in which Anglicans left the Church of England and "went over" to Rome, was also strongly abhorred by public sentiment; adherents were described as vermin gnawing away at the heart of church and state. Although the liberal prime minister William Gladstone finally repealed the Ecclesiastical Titles Act in 1871, he nonetheless still stipulated that the repeal in no way gave legal status or jurisdiction to the Roman Catholic Church in England. And in 1874, Gladstone attacked the doctrine of papal infallibility as an insult to reason and as a threat to the conjoined identity of British church and state identity. Newman attacked right back, and Gerard forever loathed Gladstone for what he perceived as opportunistic temporizing.

For all these reasons, a young Jesuit had to expect opposition, even persecution. In a governmental attempt to prohibit specifically the growth of the Society of Jesus in England, Jesuits had been forbidden by the British penal code in 1828 from swearing oaths, and this was still in effect; consequently, when Gerard and his fellow novices copied out their statement of adherence and took their vows to the Society on September 8, 1870, after the two years' novitiate, they did so secretly, in the attic.

This element of secrecy did not, however, appear to distress Gerard; in fact, it may have appealed to his personality, so prone to perceiving mystery and signs and wonders hidden beneath the crust of quotidian reality. And it is undeniable that the full flowering of his poetic endeavor did not really begin to emerge until after the novitiate, when he was sent to seminary at St. Mary's Hall in Stonyhurst, Lancashire. He departed for Stonyhurst the morning after taking his vows.

Gerard began consistently to write detailed, evocative descriptions of a spiritually charged natural world at this time. Increasingly, he seems to have resorted to his journals for the only private time and space he could find in the otherwise tightly regulated days at seminary. In part, this more programmatic approach to writing about nature, its beauties and secrets and spiritual sense, may have been provoked by the fact that, for really the first time in his life, Gerard was not living in a city or the Victorian equivalent of a suburb; with the exception of a few weekend hikes outside of Oxford or visits to the sea with his family, other than the rugged and, to him, unprecedented landscape of Switzerland, Gerard had never spent much time in the country. And now he lived deep within it. He recalled the individual particularity of entities in nature, worthy and noble without human intervention or recognition, that he had found in his epiphany in the Swiss mountains, confiding to his journal that "this busy working of nature wholly independent of the earth and seeming to go on in a strain of time not reckoned by our reckoning of days and years was like a new witness to God and filled me with delightful fear."[41]

Stonyhurst was very rural. Located in Lancashire, which, along with Yorkshire and Cumbria, had been recusant strongholds and outposts of traditionalist Roman Catholic faith, the 300-acre estate had been donated to the Society of Jesus in 1794; its former owner had then fled to America. The Jesuit presence comprised the parish church of St. Peter's, the preparatory school of St. Mary's, and the sixteenth-century manor house where Gerard attended seminary classes. The buildings were set in the woods and reached by parallel paths that crisscrossed the forest. These paths were called the Brothers' Walk, and the young Jesuits who traversed them were expected to recite portions of Ignatius's *Spiritual Exercises* as they walked along. They would pass by a granary and a mill; an observatory, established in the early 1800s; Pinfold Cross, with its *memento mori* urging the seminarians to spend their time prayerfully, as death might be imminent; and an ancient Anglo-Saxon monument called St. Paulinus Cross; after which they would come along the banks of the River Hodder, a clear-flowing stream dotted with dappled river rock.

Gerard's soul thrilled to the setting. His ever-present love for trees flourished here, and he began to express proto-environmental sentiments in his journals that would emerge more fully in later poetry, as in "Binsey Poplars," when he rebelled against the clear-cutting of a stand of poplars in a nearby yard: "My aspens dear, whose airy cages quelled, / Quelled or quenched in leaves the leaping sun, / Áll félled, félled, are áll félled; / Of a fresh and following folded rank / Not spared, not one . . . / O if we but knew what we do / When we delve or hew— / Hack and rack the growing green!"[42] Or in "Inversnaid," prompted by a trip to Scotland: "What would the world be, once bereft / Of wet and of wildness? Let them be left, / O let them be left, wildness and wet; / Long live the weeds and the wilderness yet."[43]

And already, even during seminary formation, Gerard was showing signs of the mystic's swerve from doctrine and dogma; the terms "delve" and "hew" recall Adam delving, or toiling in the fields, while Eve span, or plied her distaff, and the way Gerard uses them— lobbying against them—runs counter to the standard interpretation that work, and work altering nature, is man's God-given lot. Gerard was implicitly declaring an immanent presence of the divine within the trees. They should be left undisturbed; their presence enhanced the souls of those who beheld them. In 1864 Gerard had written a poem about Saint Dorothea, an early Christian martyr who had been tortured for declaring that God is everywhere and in all things. The drops of water on the lips of blue larkspurs were not dew, she declared, but rather stars; she thereby "linkèd heavens with milky ways," and her "sweet soul" was in death itself transmuted into astral body, "sphered so fast."[44] Gerard was beginning to develop his voice, his cosmic decodings, his spiritual certainties, the theophanies that had always been there, in his journal as a seminarian.

It is actually striking, even somewhat surprising, how little he spoke of his training as a Jesuit, of the content of his seminary studies, even of his interactions with faculty and other students. He made the rare glancing comment in his journals, noting that he was censured for having used the word "sweetheart" in a sermon and required to submit subsequent sermons in draft form to a senior Jesuit for approval. He recalled drinking "Lenten chocolate" with the other students; he had conversations with the gardeners; and he registered an occasional historical occurrence, such as Paris having been seized by the Commune. But on the whole, his journals displayed the same preoccupation with natural phenomena and the meticulous attention to detail in the description of them that they had formerly displayed—only more so. It is almost as though Gerard were seeking consolation for the deprivation of the gratification of his physical senses throughout the Jesuit formation process by resorting to the natural world. On September 24, 1870, having newly arrived at Stonyhurst, rather than bemoan the coldness of the uncarpeted floors or the frozen water in his washbasin each morning, Gerard rhapsodized about his first sight ever of the northern lights.[45]

What Pater and Ruskin had taught him about the discipline and joy derived from finding the exact word, the right phrase, the perfect adjective to evoke a wave, or a blade of grass, or the curl of a lock of hair twined about an ear ("as the leaves of a filbert . . . upon the nut"),[46] Gerard now implemented even more assiduously. Rather than discuss theology or recount ecclesiasti-

cal history, as might be expected of one who had so thoroughly
launched himself into a new life, this vocation, Gerard gave himself over more and more fully to his search for ultimate meaning
in an immanentist[47] apprehension of nature.

Nature seemed his trusted confidante, his most intimate interlocutor especially; as Gerard was increasingly coming to perceive, nature offered the highway to God. His journals show more
and more notations of conjunctions and simultaneities, of syn-
chronicities and serendipities in the natural world, of exquisite
and minute detail that pointed to a larger Presence. One journal
entry sketched "two large planets, the one an evening star, the
other distant today from it as in the diagram, both nearly of an
altitude and of one size—such counterparts that each seems the
reflection of the other in opposite bays of the sky and not two
distinct things";[48] the search for "counterparts" and "reflections"
suggests a lonely wish for a kindred soul, for a relationship and a
reciprocity lacking in Gerard's outer life but abundantly evident
in the responsiveness of nature.

Gerard began to record his dreams, many of them saturated
with strange symbolism, and he strove to project his dream images onto what he saw in reality, trying to coax another sort of
conjunction, or parallel reality—perhaps a compensatory mech-
anism for some disappointment or distress. He said, "the eye
in its sane waking office kens only impressions brought from
without.... Nevertheless I have seen in favourable moments the
images brought from within lying there like others: if I am not
mistaken they are coarser and simpler and something like the
spectra made by bright things looked hard at." He was clearly
stressed; the experiment with optics, conjoining dream and real
worlds, suggested a hallucination: "As Father Rector was giving
the points for meditation I shut my eyes, being very tired.... The
dream-images seemed to rise and overlie those which belonged
to what he was saying and I saw one of the Apostles—he was
talking about the Apostles—as if pressed against by a piece of

wood about half a yard long and a few inches across, like a long
box with two of the long sides cut off. Even then I could not understand what the piece of wood did encumbering the apostle."[49]
Shortly after this vivid, almost delusional, deeply detailed vision,
Gerard suffered some form of nervous collapse:[50] "One day in
the Long Retreat (which ended on Christmas Day) they were
reading in the refectory Sister Emmerich's account of the Agony
in the Garden and I suddenly began to cry and sob and could
not stop. I put it down for this reason, that if I had been asked
a minute beforehand I should have said that nothing of the sort
was going to happen and even when it did I stood in a manner
wondering at myself not seeing in my reason the traces of an adequate cause for such strong emotion . . . but there is always one
touch, something striking sideways and unlooked for, which . . .
undoes resistance and pierces."[51] Gerard's immediate disassocia-
tion from his emotional event ("I stood in a manner wondering at
myself"), coupled with his struggle to find a rational explanation
and then his acceptance of acute sensitivity as the cause ("there
is always one touch, something striking sideways and unlooked
for, which . . . pierces"), attests to how very unsettling he found
this occurrence. And yet such occasions began to proliferate.

The intensity with which he was drawn to natural beauty
could prove problematic for him. Aware of how strongly he
yearned for beauty, he at times imposed on himself the "penance
of the eyes" that he had practiced prior to his conversion, not
allowing himself to raise his eyes from the ground for months
at a time, in order to school himself to attend to more prosaic
occupations. During the novitiate at Roehampton, he had noted
in 1869, "Some primroses out. But a penance which I was doing
from Jan. 25 to July 25 prevented my seeing much that half-year."
Natural beauty could spur lust, prove a lure. He later noted:
"What you look hard at seems to look hard at you, hence the
true and the false instress of nature."[52] Gerard still had within
him the schoolboy who, on a dare, had abstained from water for

a month to prove his heroic capacity for self-denial. But, even more telling, he also had a deep, inner distrust of himself and of his desires. This self-distrust would haunt him all his brief life.

The poet who would not allow himself to pen verse found his sentiment of beauty overflowing into the prose of his journal. It needed an outlet. And Gerard really was incapable of bridling his urge to look, to see into the essence of things, to discern their inner hiddenness; he penetrated into mystery, and, as he did so, he was himself in some way transformed. "One day early in March . . . I looked long up at [a white streamer of cloud] till the tall height and the beauty of the scaping—regularly curled knots springing if I remember from fine stems, like foliation in wood or stone—had strongly grown on me. It changed beautiful changes."[53] He had, in a manner of speaking, incorporated the cloud. And he was perceiving synesthetically—what he saw also elicited music and aural harmony ("changed beautiful changes").[54]

There are numerous neurological explanations for this form of experiencing, and they can range from autism to epilepsy to brain tumors; some psychiatric states, as well as migraines, can also account for hallucinations and a heightened sense of reality.[55] But, as with any altered state, to some degree what matters is not their cause but rather the effect they have in providing the individual with a new, intensely personal way of apprehending the world. And, in any event, the majority of such diagnostic criteria was not available to Victorian England. What was happening—and this is key for his later poetry—is that Gerard was becoming, however inadvertently or unintentionally, an ecstatic, one who entered into and took on the life around him in an imagined, artistic creation of a new form of participation in essence. He could not help it; he practiced this urge almost mediumistically,[56] channeling what he saw into his prose descriptions that would one day overflow into the odd, weirdly rhythmed, complex compression of his poetry.

This inner capacity for outer sight coupled with a participa-

tory imagining of the hidden life of things became his customary
frame of reference, an aid and an assist: "Unless you refresh the
mind from time to time you cannot always remember or believe
how deep the inscape in things is.... [In walking and looking at
hedge banks] I could find a square scaping which helped the eye
over another hitherto disordered field of things." Gerard became
an adept, able to access this technique, a sort of meditation or
contemplation that fed his art, enabling him to intuit very fine
differences and shadings and gradations: "End of March and beginning of April—This is the time to study inscape in the spraying
of trees, for the swelling buds carry them to a pitch which the
eye could not else gather—for out of much much more, out of
little not much, out of nothing nothing: in these sprays at all
events there is a new world of inscape."[57] He also began to read
something into his scriptural lessons, as in the description above,
where Gerard creatively reworked one of Jesus's parables having
to do with "from he who has much, much is required" ("for out
of much much more...").[58]

Here, rather than describe the state of man's soul and the path
to salvation being intimated in the parable, Gerard deflected the
focus toward the saturation of the natural world with the divine.
The flowers in bud were every bit as significant as the soul of a
man, for Gerard: "in these sprays there is a new world." He was
stretching beyond flat and formulaic piety to a multidimensional
understanding.[59] He began to perceive a whole world contained
in the most miniature aspects of nature, and he sensed acute and
minute variations among all things that set his soul vibrating and
his pen stretching to describe them. It seems that the strain of
rank-and-file formation as a Jesuit paradoxically served to wrap a
pressure point around Gerard's creativity that intensified these experiences, rather than curtailed them. They would shine forth.

And all this time, during the daily grind of seminary, the
dreary visits to parishes populated by dirty, ill-clad Irish immigrants—Lancashire's population had nearly doubled in 1847 with

starving souls fleeing the potato famine—with the tedium of performing assigned tasks, such as house porter, Gerard was being prepared in a way the Jesuit fathers probably had not intended: willy-nilly, he was being shaped for his poetic endeavor. He would finally find the theological justification for his exultation over the particularities of each natural thing, his conviction that the divine dwelled within each creature, in late summer of 1872, while perusing the shelves of the Arundell Library.

Arundell was a treasure trove. Built as part of the original sixteenth-century manor house and designated as the seminary library in 1837, it contained roll after roll of medieval manuscripts, the entire archives of the English Province of the Society of Jesus, the letters of the martyred recusant Saint Edmund Campion (about whom Gerard was later to write a poem) along with the actual bloodied ropes that had been used to torture and quarter Campion, a first folio of Shakespeare, and one day, many years along, it would acquire holograph copies of all of Gerard's own correspondence and drafts.

That day, Gerard took up a book by Scotus. It was Scotus's *Oxford Commentaries* on Peter Lombard's *Sentences*. The brilliant Franciscan Scotus, who had lectured at Oxford in the twelfth century to packed rooms of adulating students seated on hay bales and straw for lack of benches, appealed to Gerard as a kindred spirit. Much as Newman's life had seemed to Gerard to map out the inevitable trajectory of Gerard's own, enabling him to approach Newman with queries and concerns he had not been fully able to voice to anyone else, or much as the diminutive poet Keats, himself from Hampstead, like Gerard, and dogged also by a sense of poetic vocation to do something quite extraordinary, was also in some ways a role model for Gerard, Gerard now felt his own responses to nature and his own theories about the relationship of God to the world validated by Scotus and by Scotus's lifting up of the individual and the particular above the general. Even Scotus's formulations, quintessentially medieval in their propositional form, came in for some imitation by Gerard, when he later composed poetical titles about theological concepts (such as "That Nature Is a Heraclitean Fire . . ." or "The Blessed Virgin Compared to the Air We Breathe").

The Aquinas he had learned at seminary, *magister* of hierarchy of being, who taught that there were ladders of meaning all along the way to God—that insects possessed less of God than horses, and horses had less than people—those teachings of Aquinas[60] were countered by Scotus's assertion of full Presence, the All in all, without hierarchy or graded distribution of meaning or worth. Gerard found the theory for his own abiding certainty that the grandeur of God, before which he was rapt, "all lost in wonder," could be concealed in the tiniest particle of nature: "Jesu whom I look at veilèd here below," also translated as "Godhead here in hiding."[61] Gerard exulted to his journal the day he began to read Scotus, this new soulmate: "I was flush with a new stroke of enthusiasm. It may come to nothing or it may be a mercy from God."[62] Scotus suggested to Gerard how, with this beauty of the Lancashire countryside flooding his senses, Gerard could liberate himself from the conventional wisdom that focus on the material world hampered concentration on heaven.

Gerard's encounter with Scotus proved transformative in that it provided him with the intellectual impetus and theological warrant to move forward in a new direction.[63] He was ready. Already he was raising eyebrows at seminary for the quirky way in which he made the *Spiritual Exercises*. Ignatius had recommended that the reader take each scenario and insert himself within it as if a spectator at the theater. He was to act as if he were there, beholding the passion of Christ, or the shepherds at the manger, or any other event in Christ's life. The exercitant making the *Exercises* was supposed to imagine himself within that event and then derive a spiritual message from that willed involvement. But Gerard did it differently, as, it seems, he did most things. As well as draw a deeper meaning about Christ from the set scenario,

Gerard sought crucial clarity about his own identity in Christ, what he began to call "selfbeing," the inscape of man.[64]

At a retreat some years later at Liverpool in 1880, Gerard's notes reflecting on the exercise offer an example of the unusual application he was making of it. He did not remain meditating on the prescribed scene but rather swerved off of it, to explore himself more deeply, to find his own inscape as he also found inscapes in nature:

> When I consider my selfbeing, my consciousness and feel-
> ing of myself, that taste of myself, of *I* and *me* above and in
> all things, which is more distinctive than the taste of ale or
> alum, more distinctive than the smell of walnutleaf or cam-
> phor, and is incommunicable by any means to another man
> (as when I was a child I used to ask myself: What must it
> be to be someone else?). Nothing else in nature comes near
> this unspeakable stress of pitch, distinctiveness, and selving,
> this selfbeing of my own. Nothing explains it or resembles it,
> except so far as this, that other men to themselves have the
> same feeling. But this only multiplies the phenomena to be
> explained so far as the cases are like and do resemble.[65]

His language was, again, synesthetic ("that taste of myself"; "the smell of walnutleaf or camphor"), and his sense of the interpenetration of all reality within and available to the self from without ("of *I* and *me* above and in all things"), and the urgings of empathy in fathoming the secrets of other beings ("What must it be to be someone else?"), were richly developed. His journal entry offered a theory in germ of how his poetry would enlarge the bounds of identification with another through a mutuality, resemblance, imagined entry into another ("so far as the cases are like and do resemble"). Selfbeing, like inscape, had become a penetration of essence, a drama and an event—but not the drama he was assigned to meditate on. Or, indeed, that same drama, but as Gerard himself saw it, solely saw it, in and through his own very uniquely fashioned soul and personality. Gerard's journal response to the Ignatian exercise had wandered far from its set task: to consider "Homo creatus est: how man was created to praise, reverence and serve God Our Lord, and by so doing to save his soul." This was deep and vagabond contemplation; it was not controllable. This was not what Ignatius had envisioned.

When one's most cherished inner thoughts cannot be shared with others, when one lacks a confidant, the pressure to communicate seeks a new outlet. Poetry ranked highest, even above music and art, in Gerard's personal pantheon of arts conveying beauty, and so it was inevitable that he would begin to write again one day. He perceived as a privileged observer, the necessary transcriber of marvel and miracle hidden in everyday housing. He saw himself as the one to whom God's glory was made most manifest: "I wálk, I líft up, Í lift úp heart, éyes, / Down all that glory in the heavens to glean our Saviour." "These things, these things were here and but the beholder / Wánting"[66]—"wanting," that is, were not he, Gerard, there to observe and record them. His journals brimmed and bristled with energetic, evocative prose replete with the movement of present participles;[67] appropriately, too, as so much of his observation had to do with phenomena such as changing clouds, his journals were characterized by kaleidoscopic shifts of waves and rivulets, certain slants of light: "such a lovely *damasking* in the sky as today I never felt before. The blue was charged with simple instress, the higher, zenith sky earnest and *frowning*, lower more light and sweet. High up again, *breathing* through woolly coats of cloud . . . it was the true exchange of crimson . . . in the opposite south-western bay below the sun it was . . . shaken over with slanted *flashing* 'travellers,' all in flight, *stepping* one behind the other . . . all in a scale down the air *falling* one after the other to the ground."[68] The step from such prose as this to verse requires hardly even a tiny shuffle. In the meantime, Gerard stored his perceptions up and pondered them.

A sickly seminarian, Gerard had been suffering from colds and flus and eczema during the three years at Stonyhurst, and he was forbidden by his superior from fasting during Lent of 1873 lest his health be imperiled. So he stayed indoors and turned inward to read Scotus, a good book to ruminate on, a thinker whose theology made sense to him. Scotus had been born in England, had trained and taught at Oxford, and professed a special devotion, as did Gerard, to the Blessed Mother. The doctrine of the Immaculate Conception had formally received papal sanction under Pius IX (*Ineffabilus Deus*) only fairly recently, on December 8, 1854, and all the more strongly did Gerard embrace it. Further, Scotus had taught that atonement theology was beside the point; the incarnation *could have* and *would have* taken place *independently* of Adam's fall and consequent need for redemption.

Rather than the traditional avenging God who must be appeased through blood sacrifice, Scotus talked of a loving and lovable God who, understanding *humans'* perceived need for propitiation (rather than God's insistence on it), himself decided to be the blood sacrifice, an ultimate form of *kenosis*, or gracious self-outpouring. The man-God died on the cross in the form of man so that humanity could perceive and understand it; but the true sacrifice was God undoing God's self on the cross. Now a will to love could enter into the human heart, and a freedom from fear and guilt ensue.[69]

Further, such an act of divine self-abasement graced the entire created order, recognizing it as so infinitely lovable and worthwhile that it could now be regarded without skepticism or suspicion. Materiality could be a privileged vessel for the indwelling of God. Nature was indeed valuable, as Gerard had sensed. And his poetry in this way, and through the application of Scotus's theology, began to become for Gerard a "sacramental"—not a sacrament, or visible sign of an invisible Reality, as Augustine had defined it, but rather a *sacramental*, as the Roman Catholic Church acknowledged it. A "sacramental" was not sacred in and of itself. It was, rather, an evolved means by and through which

God could be perceived, a practice or an observance analogous to, but not itself deemed to be, a sacrament. A "sacramental" understanding freed Gerard legitimately to view virtually any creature of nature as an avenue for apprehending the Divine: "There is scarcely any proper use of material things which cannot thus be directed toward the sanctification of men and the praise of God."[70]

By stressing the utter freedom of the incarnation, untethered to any program to save humanity, Scotus was issuing a full invitation to all of creation to participate in the incarnation. Christ as a human came in order that he might be a sort of sensory envelope for the divine, so that God could experience his world as his creatures did. In wanting that full connection, God chose Christ to be not only an intermediary but also a full participant—in both the human and the divine reality—in a sort of cosmic call-and-response that explained for Gerard how the created world displayed seeds and signs of the divine. Christ's enfleshment showed that the world of the senses was not scorned by the Father. Quotidian reality could indeed be a privileged medium to epitomize and evoke divinity. So much of Gerard's interior struggling, and wrestling with what he had been taught, abated; he said of Scotus, "he of all men most sways my spirit to peace."[71]

Gerard may have found other volumes on the long, wooden library shelves. These would have spoken of *theōsis*, the progressive divinization of all creation. Early Eastern fathers such as Gregory of Nyssa and Basil of Caesarea, the Cappadocian fathers,[72] known for their capacious understanding of the value of every creature,[73] or the mystical writings of Symeon the New Theologian, Ephrem the Syrian, and Maximus the Confessor made the case for the cosmic Christ, Redeemer of all, both man and nonhuman animal. While the Greek patristics may not have been featured in the Jesuit curriculum—the first year was Aquinas, Catholic doctrine, and mathematics; the second and third years featured some science (primarily mechanics), ethics, but also "special metaphysics"—they were surely available in the library, perhaps in relation to this latter category of metaphysics, and Gerard was also obviously reading widely on a self-directed, individual program.

But what seems most to have appealed to Gerard, in any event, was Scotus's notion that Christ was a sort of *sensorium*, or experiential envelope, for God: Christ was God's way of experiencing what it was like to be human, to be in God's world. This meant that, were Gerard to concentrate enough on, and observe sufficiently closely, the elements of natural beauty that so attracted him, Gerard could comprehend the mind of God: he could intuit how God was not only revealed in, but also how God *felt* in, a particular creature. Scotus gave back to Gerard the senses, legitimized, that Gerard, in his excessive scrupulosity, had viewed with such suspicion and had even, in his earlier Savanarolesque bonfire of the verses, sought to eradicate.

The problem was, as with Gerard's rather quixotic stabs at Ignatian reflection, his Jesuit superiors for the most part took a dim view. It was probably more the case that they did not approve of the use to which Gerard was putting his new knowledge; they were certainly already beginning to wonder where an appropriate posting for the eccentric young man might be found. Further, while Scotist thought was discussed at seminary—Faber's Scotus-influenced (he agreed with Scotus that, even had Adam not fallen, Christ would still have come into the world) *The Creature and the Creator* was read aloud in excerpts at the refectory table—Aquinas was canonical; while Jesuits certainly were informed of Scotus's theology, and while Suarez put forward a modified version of it, their curriculum centered more on Aquinas.[74]

Scotus's idea of *haeccitas*[75] postulated that individual essence was known in God's mind prior to the actual creation of the entity to bear that essence. This was an elevation of the distinct uniqueness of all creatures to a status never before fully expressed in Western theology (although developed by mystics such as the

Dominican Meister Eckhart): if that essence preresided in God's mind, that essence made of each creature an exceptionally singular thought of God, a manifestation of his loving, creative will. Each essence was, in effect, an *idea* of God subsequently embodied in concrete and individual, not abstract and general, form. Scotus had stated unequivocally, "God knows all creatures."[76]

In a manner of speaking, Darwin's current and controversial, especially for some churchmen, study of species treated the individual as significant only as part of a process. Gerard's traditionalism, as well as his artistic temperament, inclined him to value the individual over the species. The more Gerard became entranced with Scotus, the more he slipped free rein to his idiosyncratic impulses to study nature, to commune with it, to hear it speaking in God's voice.

At this time Gerard also was curious about miracles and signs, believing that he had "ears to hear and eyes to see." Like many Victorians, Gerard thought that fetches and fairies and ghosts might exist;[77] he gave credence to messages communicated by signs and wonders ("It is about the seventh time that I think I have had some token from heaven," he confided to his journal), and he intended to cultivate and refine his ability to receive more such signs: the star seen by the Magi, he said, "was nothing to ordinary observers, perhaps not visible at all to them."[78] In this way he equated himself with magicians and thaumaturges. Both Gerard's personal eccentricities—which, through his reading of Scotus, Gerard could now construe as his own, distinct, "Gerard-ness" willed for him by God—and his erratic theological training came in for worried scrutiny on his superiors' part.

It may have been more the application that Gerard was making of Scotus that concerned Gerard's seminary professors, because he was more and more constructing a world of his own. By nature obsessive, he fixated on anything he could find to feed into his enthrallment with the natural world as a revelation of the divine. He wrote in his journal on August 3, 1872, that "when I took in any inscape of the sky or sea I thought of Scotus."[79] His journals burst with details and eclectic observations, as though he were cramming full a memory book of all his experiences and reflections, a storehouse of his hidden self lying in wait for the proper time. "No one knows where I may break out next," he said.[80]

On a visit to the Oratory in July the following year, Gerard was thrilled to make the acquaintance of David Lewis and Brande Morris, whom he deemed "two, and I suppose the only two Scotists in England."[81] He was finding a small circle of like-minded people to bolster his enthusiasm for Scotus. Lewis had converted to Roman Catholicism and then had served as Newman's curate at St. Mary's. Newman had been taught Scotus's view on the incarnation by his bishop, Ulathorne of Birmingham, at the time that Newman founded the Oratory. Newman had also advocated some version of Scotism in his translation of Athanasius when he maintained that the incarnation occurred independently of Adam's sin. And Newman had spoken favorably earlier to Hopkins of how the Jesuits avoided an extreme form of Thomism.[82] As for Morris, whom friends teasingly dubbed "Simeon Stylites" (a pillar-dwelling desert father of the early Christian church) for his reluctance to leave the Exeter tower room in which he spent most of his time reading, he became a patristics scholar and converted to Roman Catholicism. He wrote a two-volume *Doctrine of the Catholic Church* (1851) that showed Scotus's influence, most notably in his discussion of whether the Christ would have been incarnate even without the fall of Adam. Gerard's meeting with Morris further points to Gerard's awareness of the Greek patristic writers, as Morris was, in fact, the translator of the Greek theologian Ephrem the Syrian.

Gerard was developing a sort of fixation with Scotus, which was not the purpose for theological education that the Jesuits had envisioned in his formative process. His superiors, concerned about both Gerard's mental and physical state, sent him away to London, where he was to teach Latin, English, and Greek to the juniors, a fairly nondemanding appointment designed to give him a change of venue and an opportunity to rest and restore his health.

Yet, while in London, Gerard continued to stoke his growing excitement and sense of a way forward through Scotus by developing a correspondence with Mandell Creighton. Creighton was an Anglican clergyman and parish priest, who later became bishop of Peterborough in 1891 and then bishop of London in 1897. He also held an endowed chair in ecclesiastical history at Cambridge. However, their connection was long-standing; it went back to Gerard's Oxford days when he had known Creighton, who was only a year older than Gerard. Creighton had been a popular and very intellectual boy dubbed "the Professor" by his fellow students, a Merton College matriculator, one of Jowett's pupils, and a staunch member of the devout club called the Quadrilateral.[83] Like Gerard, too, Creighton was somewhat of an aesthete, venerating Pater, Ruskin, and William Morris and the arts and crafts movement of the day.

So there were commonalities, a shared history at Oxford, and, in addition, Gerard trusted Creighton and admired his scholarship. Further, Creighton was quite reliably High Church; he had taken holy orders in 1870, had married, then taught at Oxford, helping out with preaching at St. Gilles Church in 1873. On Easter Day 1875 he had begun a rectorship in Embledon, Northumbria, a village along a ridge of basalt rock overlooking the sea and comprising some six hundred very rural souls; he was a firm upholder of the Anglican church and state correlation, and a likely contender for the position of archbishop of Canterbury. Creighton had declined to read Darwin because he deemed it purely conjectural and therefore not of interest to him. Creighton preferred concrete over abstract reasoning, also like Gerard and Scotus. Gerard wrote to Creighton, a scholar of the Renaissance papacy who was also conversant in earlier theology, to get more information about Scotus.[84]

Gerard was to establish epistolary relationships with two other chief interlocutors of his adult life, Bridges and Dixon. Gerard had begun his correspondence with Bridges while still an undergraduate, and it continued throughout his Jesuit formation—with some hitches and stutters particularly during the novitiate, when Bridges rebelled against the custom of a superior opening and censoring the letters Gerard sent as well as received.[85] Gerard did not initiate his correspondence with Dixon until his time in Ireland. However, the epistolary relationship with Creighton anticipated these other close relationships through correspondence that would provide welcome, critical reflection on Gerard's poetical project.

It was not uncommon for Victorian men and women to sustain voluminous correspondence; what is striking in Gerard's case is that, after his time at Oxford, he saw Bridges only a few more times while in London, and he met with Dixon only once as an adult.[86] He was so solitary—in part because of the demands of the Society of Jesus, at times because of what seemed a mounting melancholia, and also because, apparently, ideas mattered to him more than personalities—that he had very little actual interaction with major figures in his life. But all three of these correspondents came from Gerard's early days. Dixon had been a form master at Gerard's preparatory school, Highgate, and Bridges and Creighton were both from his Oxford days. And these three correspondents were all Anglican, not Roman Catholic. It is as though, both formed and thwarted as a Jesuit, Gerard was going back to his younger days to pick up the pieces of a life he had only partly lived.

He did, at least at first, seem partly liberated from the serious Gerard of seminary days during his time in London. He went to several art exhibitions, at times accompanied by his brother Arthur, took notes on the pictures that struck him as manifesting inscape and instress, and also attempted to learn to play the piano. He also took a holiday in Devon, where Coleridge had lived, a rural area where tin mines dotted the landscape inland from the coast. Gerard roamed Devon's cliffs and sandy shores, stopping in seaside resorts.

But his mood was troubled, and he was tired and sad. Although he found seminary stressful, he also found its structure and ordered days psychologically soothing. Newman had told him this would be so. Now in London and away from the countryside, briefly, intermittently, Gerard's joy in the world around him receded and he wrote, "Being unwell I was quite downcast; nature in all her parcels and faculties gaped and fell apart like a clod heaving and holding only by strings of root."[87]

A change was coming; it was needed, he felt. But this change was not to be of his choosing. In August 1874, his Jesuit superiors decided to send Gerard to St. Beuno's in Wales, where his training in theology would continue and where he could take a break from teaching.

CHAPTER 3   ILLUMINATION

*Place the whole affection on the Creator, loving
Him in all creatures.*[1]

*God knows infinite things, all things, and heeds
them all in particular.*[2]

GERARD WAS SENT to St. Beuno's in Denbighshire, Wales.[3]
St. Beuno's had sweeping views of the wind-wracked Snowdo-
nia mountains and also of the northern coast. Wales was still
very wild, with many walking paths and hiking trails to scenic
natural attractions, such as the austere Mount Snowdon. Local
towns displayed wattle and timber architecture, with low, heavy
beams and whitewashing, very medieval in appearance. The Jesuit school had been built in 1848 on the model of a small university college to provide an outlet for the increasing numbers of
priestly aspirants applying to the Society of Jesus who needed to
be educated and formed in the faith. Built by the famed archi-
tect Joseph Aloysius Hansom (1803–1882), St. Beuno's had many
small rooms and large corridors, and featured elaborate stained-
glass windows, but was otherwise, as Gerard observed, "skimping
within"; the building had no source of heat other than that generated by open fires, although an ingenious heat exchange system
moved warmer air from the greenhouse into the main building.
Water came from a nearby stream, and produce for the refectory
table was grown on the grounds. Students and professors lodged
in the larger galleries to the south of the house.

Throughout the United Kingdom, as the Catholic Church

designated parochial jurisdictions under Pius IX's programmatic reforms and sought to reestablish a permanent, institutional footing, Roman Catholic schools, churches, and convents in the Gothic Revival style were springing up, most of them due to the visionary architecture of Hansom, son of a Yorkshire Catholic recusant family.[4] An intense, thin, heavily mustachioed man, he also invented the hansom cab and started the well-known architectural journal the *Builder*. After receiving the commission to build the Birmingham Town Hall, and after having gone into bankruptcy due to unpaid receipts from builders for whom he had stood surety, he became a socialist and allied his cause with one of Gerard's heroes, Robert Owen, the Welsh textile manufacturer and founder of the utopian community of New Harmony, Indiana.[5] Hansom designed and built for Owen Queenwood College, the site of Owen's final, abortive effort to establish a cooperative living experience. Hansom also built the Oxford Oratory, modeled on Cardinal Newman's Birmingham Oratory. Subsequently, perhaps because of family and ecclesiastical contacts, Hansom worked primarily for the Society of Jesus or for Catholic gentry, descendants of recusants, building in the Gothic Revival idiom (with details of his own devising, such as the hammer beam ceiling or, at St. Walburge's in Preston, the single highest church steeple in all of England) and, later, the ornate French Revival style with ogive windows and flying buttresses.

Gerard was to worship and serve at the smallest cathedral in the United Kingdom, the grey stone Cathedral of St. Asaph, some 1,200 years old at the time. From there he could visit St. Winefred's Well in nearby Flintshire, site of the oldest pilgrimage in Great Britain, dating to a sixth-century martyr who was memorialized in the sixteenth century and whose story he was later to dramatize in verse. Wales was predominantly Anglican, and the populace referred to Roman Catholic churches pejoratively as "chapels."[6] But the British provincial of the Jesuits, Father Randal Lythgoe, toured some landholdings in local

Tremerchion and determined to situate St. Beuno's there in the rural Welsh countryside, believed to be healthier, removed from the sources of typhoid and cholera in the cities.

Wales, for Gerard, was both a spiritual homecoming of sorts and a literary revelation. Although the landscape was not pristine—none of the countryside in Great Britain had been entirely spared the ravages of industrialism, and ironworks, and tin, slate, and coal pits, pocked the land—Wales was nonetheless in many areas beautiful and bucolic, with canal towpaths and castle ruins, and green, green everywhere, fields and hillocks spotted with white sheep and Guernsey cows. Gerard was to be happier there than at any time in his life. Accompanied by his friends, novices Henry and William Kerr, Gerard loved to ramble about Wales, bathing himself in natural beauty. They wandered innumerable footpaths, Gerard with his wide-brimmed straw hat securely fastened under his dimpled chin with a ribbon, portable paint-box and sketchpad in his rucksack jumbled together with a pocket-sized lined journal and a stub of a pencil for jotting notes. Gerard observed the world without as he built his world within. In observing the natural world, he was observing God's effects, Scotus had taught him, so what he contemplated *was* ultimately God.

He spent from 1874 to 1877 at St. Beuno's, and it was here that he, at last, in December of 1875, felt himself "given leave" to again write poetry. It was a landscape that had inspired other poets, such as Wordsworth, who wrote "Lines Written a Few Miles above Tintern Abbey" after his trip to Chepstow, Wales—and that would continue to inspire poets, like Dylan Thomas, from Swansea. But for Gerard the inspiration was deeply theological as well as literary.[7] He discerned God in the lineaments of this landscape, its monuments and megaliths, meadows and mountains. He wrote, "Since, though he is under the world's splendour and wonder, / His mystery must be instressed, stressed; / For I greet him the days I meet him, and bless when I understand."[8] This was Gerard's own, personal language of theological encounter, and it may be translated in this way: "instressed" indicated Christ indwelling the local habitations, while "stressed" showed Christ received, in, under, and through that manifestation, into Gerard's heart.

Some of Gerard's ancestors on his mother's side had been Welsh, so Gerard identified strongly with the local folk: "I have always looked on myself as half Welsh," he confided.[9] In Wales, he encountered an entirely different language, with unusual intonations and accents, and a well-developed body of poetry and song. The Jesuits frowned on languages being learned merely for amusement or pleasure, however, and he was quickly told that he was only to learn the language if he intended to use it to missionize, preach, or catechize.[10]

Gerard enjoyed the rhythms of the Welsh language, and, in an attempt to become proficient in it, engaged as tutor a young woman named Susannah Jones, sister of John Hugh Jones, who had attended Jesus College as well as St. Beuno's and was ordained a priest in 1872.

The dancing lilt of Welsh speech seeped into Gerard's eversensitive ears, its alliteration and phrasings making his thoughts turn more and more to poetry again. When he first arrived at St. Beuno's, he had begun trying to teach himself to play the piano, thinking a good deal about chords and patterns of rhythm. The particular Welsh use of alliteration seemed musical to him, too. He found a treasure trove of poetic patterns called *cynghanedd*, one type of which used intricate clusters of repeated consonants and echoed consonants, interior rhyme all within one line, and virtuosic schemes of rhyming and stress. He wanted to experiment with this technique in verse. He explained to Dixon, "I had long had haunting my ear the echo of a new rhythm. . . . It consists in scanning by accents or stresses alone, without any account of the number of syllables. . . . There are hints of it in music, in nursery rhymes and popular jingles, in the poets themselves. . . . But no one has professedly used it and made it the principle throughout. . . .

[It has] certain chimes suggested by the Welsh poetry I had been reading."[11] *Cynghanedd*'s strict and elaborate rules of rhyming appealed to his obsessive and meticulous nature as well as spoke to his quest for the absolute. The discipline of versification required to use *cynghanedd* convinced Gerard that an exact description, a formal phrasing, of a specific creature's entity could be attained.

Scotus had argued that, as theology was the queen of all sciences, it must speak truth about God and therefore must be exquisitely sensitive to the words it used. Pater had taught Gerard at Oxford to maintain fine and precise documentation, to capture the essence of what he saw as though he were an engineer or an inventor, with every tiny detail accounted for. Gerard had learned from his reading of Ruskin to observe scrupulously and to write exact descriptions aiming at full essence, and Gerard had practiced this during his rambles and strolls at Oxford, in Switzerland, at Stonyhurst. Putting these precepts into practice *was* lived experience for Gerard; cloistered in a homosocial environment,[12] he had little experience of romantic love, and with most of his energies being engaged by teaching, preaching, and studying, he rarely consorted with the other Jesuits in any social way. Poetry offered him a voice and, through correspondence as well as prayer, Gerard found a companion to listen. Here, in Wales, Gerard's theology, technique, and practice came together in an extraordinary flowering of poetic productivity.

But it required a contemporary tragedy to jostle Gerard into poetic activity. He was given permission—indeed, he requested—to write a poem commemorating the wreck of the ship *Deutschland*, which left Bremen on December 6, 1875, and sank on the Kentish Knock sandbar in the Thames during a violent storm on December 7, 1875. Among those lost were five Franciscan nuns who had been exiled under the Falck Laws from Germany for their Roman Catholic faith and were aboard the ship headed for America. The newspaper-reading public throughout Great Britain was galvanized by the event. The *Times* recounted how "the chief sister, a gaunt woman 6ft. high, call[ed] out loudly and often 'O Christ, come quickly!' till the end came"; she, "at midnight . . . , by stand-ing on a table in the saloon, was able to thrust her body through the skylight" to be heard "above the roar of the storm."[13] What made the wreck especially tragic was that the ship ran aground close to shore, but its distress signals went undetected. Only after the force of the storm had spent itself was the ship discovered.

Gerard was moved by the plight of the nuns fleeing persecu-tion. In 1864, Pope Pius IX had vigorously denied the separation of church and state in his bull *Quanta Cura*. The newly organized, primarily Protestant German Empire, particularly the Kingdom of Prussia, in the throes of the *Kulturkampf* conflict with the Catholic Church, reacted against this proclamation with charges of ultramontanist influence. In 1871, Bismarck passed the Pulpit Law to ensure that no Roman Catholic cleric could speak publicly on political matters; by 1872 the Society of Jesus had been forbid-den from establishing new offshoots within the German Empire, and the state, under Falck, the minister of education, took over the training of all clergy. The Breadbasket Laws of 1875 removed any state support from clergy who would not acknowledge the supremacy of the state. Noncompliants were deported.[14]

Surviving eyewitnesses described the horrors of the storm and the drownings that fateful night, but they also especially praised the courage of the nuns, in particular she who braved the storm heroically, calling for Christ to come quickly so that she might join her Lord. Roman Catholics in England conceived of the Francis-can five as martyrs. Gerard, along with the other Jesuits, was deeply distressed by the nuns' fate, even more so because the Society of Jesus, like the Franciscans, had been specifically targeted by the Falck Laws.[15] They were further outraged when William Glad-stone launched a salvo against Rome with his 1874 publication of *The Vatican Decrees and Their Bearing on Civil Allegiance*.

Gerard's Jesuit superior suggested he write a poem about the disaster. This was the standard way to commemorate something significant; the poet laureate Alfred Lord Tennyson had similarly memorialized the quixotic charge of the Light Brigade, which still lives in the popular imagination. Prose was for journalism; poetry was the language of memory and great deeds. Gerard took to the task immediately, and he produced an extraordinary poem, "The Wreck of the *Deutschland*," which, because of its difficulty and stunning innovations, was never to appear in print; although Father Coleridge initially accepted it for publication in the Jesuit journal the *Month*, he subsequently rescinded the acceptance.

The poem was simply too strange. Even Gerard's friend and supporter Robert Bridges detested its oddities: "I wish those nuns had stayed at home," he grouched.[16] And much to Gerard's disgust, Bridges equated Gerard's verse with the experimentations of his dissolute contemporary, Walt Whitman. Yet today, "The Wreck of the *Deutschland*" is reckoned "one of the great liberating forces of twentieth century poetry," precisely because of its unusual rhythms and innovations.[17]

The poem was a crucible, a compression of everything Gerard had been thinking about poetry. At times autobiographical, it was also deeply confessional, a statement of faith, a political protest against persecution, and a literary tour de force. It built up the seascape with an impasto of adjectives; it was visionary like a Turner painting with fiery, strident colors and eerie sounds; and it created the extraordinary persona of the larger-than-life, Christlike, Christ-calling nun.

There are two heroes in the poem. One is a sailor, described as flush with youth and manly beauty, who ropes himself to the rigging, then reaches to save some women and children who have been swept into the sea. But he is sacrificed to the rage of the storm, killed almost instantly by a falling spar, and his body dangles, lifeless, buffeted to and fro by the winds, for the remainder of the poem. His act was courageous and compassionate, but it was futile ("What could he do?" Gerard asked rhetorically), not motivated, it seems, by faith. The figure of faith is the sailor's foil: the nun, described as inordinately tall and staunch, almost masculine in her size, a larger-than-life hero, a saint, a witness to faith and victor over her fear. She summons her Lord, recognizing that in her dying will be her life: ". . . Christ, King, Head: / . . . Do, deal, lord it with living and dead . . . / Ah! there was a heart right! / . . . [that a] Maiden could obey so, be a bell to, ring óf it."[18] Gerard portrayed her, lashed to a mast and standing, a strong bulwark, setting an example of faith for others, until her death. Her body seems a crucifixion, lifted up above the storm.

Tiny five-foot-four Gerard, frail priest, safe in his room at St. Beuno's, painted himself into the poem after the fact ("Away in the loveable west, / On a pastoral forehead of Wales, / I was under a roof here, I was at rest, / And they the prey of the gales"); yet he was doing a brave thing, too, for he turned the current event, possibly a solely secular tragedy in the eyes of the world, into a religious statement and an act of faith, an enduring representation of a strong spirit sacrificed to the injustices of both weather and persecution. In fact, he identified with the strong nun, claiming relationship through "her master and mine!" He compared his priestly vocation to her witness; he was lashed to it, under orders from Christ, facing fear down, calling out the gospel that others might hear: "I did say yes / O at lightning and lashed rod; / Thou heardst me . . . / . . . But roped with, always, all the way down . . . / [compelled to] the gospel proffer."[19]

And not only the story of what happened, but also Gerard's language as he told it, sears into the reader's imagination, scoring waves and screams and bold defiance and sobs of sorrow simultaneously into the reader's ear. The layers of sound Gerard generated to evoke the event construct a maelstrom of sensation; the reader falls into a vortex of words, finally to emerge on the far side of this poetic event, in an exhausted yet exultant resurrection. Gerard featured the Word, Christ, returning to British shores and hearts through the testimony of the nun: "Dame, at our door / Drówned, and among oúr shóals, / Remember us in the roads, the heaven-haven of the reward: / Our Kíng back, Oh, upon Énglish sóuls! / Let him easter in us."[20]

"The Wreck of the *Deutschland*," his first real poem as an adult, was a theological manifesto. It is possible, even likely, given his theological formation at the time, that he applied the Ignatian meditation technique to its composition. Ignatius had described three stages for devout contemplation: seeing the event through a process of imaginary re-creation; dramatizing the event as though one were there; and imagining the effect of the event within the theater of one's own spirit. But if Gerard used Jesuit meditational models to launch his visionary poem, he also employed Scotist Franciscan technique and focus—on the deliberate, careful, intuited extraction of each being's specific and particular identity in God.

Gerard was bringing all of his own being, all of his training, including the precise and painterly approach he had learned earlier by reading Ruskin, to bear on the poem, pressing his essence out into it, showing what he knew and what he believed. Ruskin, preeminent art critic of his day, defender of both Turner and the Pre-Raphaelites, visionary socialist, iconoclastic thinker, and prolific author,[21] had taught Gerard the art of how to look, how to think about looking, saying, "[I hope] that I may succeed in making some of you English youths like better to look at a bird than to shoot it,"[22] and he had claimed, "you think the use of cherry blossom is to produce cherries.... Not at all. It is because of its beauty that its continuance is worth Heaven's while."[23] To Gerard, Ruskin's approach complemented Scotus's theology.

In his fledgling iteration of an understanding of how theology and poetry intertwined, Gerard posited that grace touched on the essence of a man or of a creature; he called this essence the "vein of personality," as though God were taking a pulse, feeling the heartbeat. Gerard argued that each creature had the ability and even the desire to reach higher, to aspire to a greater stage, what he called a "tower" and "pitch," but that a higher grace had to be imputed to the creature to enable this transformation.

"There is a scale or range of pitch which is also infinite and terminates upwards in the directness or uprightness of the 'stem' of the godhead and the procession of the divine persons. God then can shift the self that lies in one to a higher, that is / better, pitch of itself." A special receptivity to God's transforming grace could, Gerard believed, be cultivated through meditating on beauty, prayer, good works and charitable deeds, and the imitation of heroic exemplars such as the nun, and, above all, through a casting of one's self, a honing of the aspirations, to always yearn beyond the self and toward God. "This access is either of grace, which is 'supernature,' to nature or of more grace to grace already given, and it takes the form of instressing the affective will."[24] Then communion with Christ could occur, as the "instress" of Christ was accepted, consciously "stressed."

Aquinas had famously said that grace builds on nature. But for Gerard, as for Scotus, that nature had the power, and even the need, to respond, to accept that grace willingly, to cooperate in its transformation. So the nun, in her bravery and self-surpassing, leaves her old self and moves fully into the new self she had in her sight when she first took her vows: "This shift is grace. For grace is any action, activity, on God's part by which, in creating or after creating, he carries the creature to or towards the end of its being, which is its selfsacrifice to God and its salvation."[25] The nun becomes fully herself, her most full self, known in Christ.

Typically, Gerard used a very sensual image, that of a ripe berry bursting with fluid full in the mouth, to describe how Christ's instress, once acknowledged, could flood and change a person: "How a lush-kept plush-capped sloe / Will, mouthed to flesh-burst, / Gush!—flush the man, the being with it . . . / Brim, in a flash, full!—Hither then, last or first, / To hero of Calvary, Christ,'s feet— / Never ask if meaning it, wanting it, warned of it—men go."[26] The rhythms here, and the ejaculation, were markedly similar to those in what was to be another of Gerard's greatest poems, "The Windhover," when he told how his "heart in hiding / Stirred for a bird,—the achieve of, the mastery of the thing! / Brute beauty and valour and act, oh, air, pride, plume, here / Buckle! AND the fire that breaks from thee then, a billion / Times told lovelier, more dangerous, O my chevalier!"[27] The same reaching after the right word and eventual seizing of it ("lush-kept plush-capped"; "air, pride, plume"); a similar use of exclamation points ("Gush!" "Buckle!") and a consistent intimation of danger, self-sacrifice, a trial to be endured ("never ask if meaning it, wanting it, warned of it . . . ," "a billion times . . . more dangerous"); the "chimings" of rich, consonantal echoes ("lush . . . plush . . . flush . . . gush") mutating into different vowels heard yet in similar sounds ("flesh, flash") and alliterations prompted by Welsh poetry ("Heart . . . hiding" "brute beauty . . . breaks . . . buckle . . . billion"); these shared traits show that Gerard was developing a twinned poetic and theological statement of faith, as well as a method for how to attain that.

"The Windhover" attests to the ongoing, intentional elucidation and illustration of this manifesto begun in "The Wreck of the *Deutschland*." The poem moves us precisely because of its intense, concentrated particularity. This is Scotist: the windhover is truly hawk, gliding on the up-currents; that the bird, in the beauty of doing the very thing that he does naturally—that is, in his God-given essence—happens to elevate our hearts ("AND the fire that breaks from thee then") is a wonder and a blessing but also, in some way, secondary to the grandeur of the hawk's smooth soaring. We would not be so moved were the windhover in any way diminished in his natural self. Like the tall nun, the windhover pierces the sky and inhabits a higher realm; like the nun, he draws our eyes to him; like the nun, he is transformed. He flashes with fire, the fire that resides at the heart of burning coals ("Blue-bleak embers . . . gásh góld-vermílion"),[28] the fire that calcines and purifies our soul in a spiritual alchemy. And yet, this is a purely natural phenomenon, just as the nun's decision to stand firm is a self-willed choice natural to the essence of who she is: "no wónder of it,"[29] Gerard demurred. Just so, the hawk calls to our soul because he is who, and how, he is—purely, simply, without reflection. The windhover demonstrates that in specific, definable particularity, mystery still remains, and that mystery leads to a sense of cosmic connection and a continued wonderment, a willed self-surpassing. The cruciform shadow of the hovering wings as the hawk swoops from heaven to skim the surface of the earth was, for Gerard, a figuration of the incarnate Christ.

Sight, and wonderment, fused for Gerard with artistic technique and Scotist focus on particularity. Ruskin had taught the optics of vision, the art of seeing through and beyond. In *Modern Painters* (1843), volume 1, which Gerard had read avidly, Ruskin had counseled,

> Changes like these, and states of vision corresponding to them, take place with each and all of the objects of nature. . . . First, place an object as close to the eye as you like, there is always something in it which you *cannot* see. . . . Secondly, place an object as far from the eye as you like, and until it becomes itself a mere spot, there is always something in it which you *can* see. . . . And thus nature is never distinct and never vacant, she is always mysterious, but always abundant; you always see something but you never see all.[30]

Scotus might have put the same realization this way: Each individual, every experience, was unique and could never be exactly replicated; in part this is because God, who, as Gerard said, "fathers-forth whose beauty is pást change,"[31] was yet ever creating, ever effecting change in the world; therefore, an untold number of possible encounters might arise that could, in turn, change the viewer. This is, in spiritual terms, a description of mystic experience. And such an experience is available to all who seek it, which is what the Scotist dimension proclaims: in our very ordinariness, the potential for this utter beauty, this miracle, resides ("shéer plód makes plóugh down síllion / Shine").[32] "Everything finite, since it is less than the infinite, represents a part of divinity."[33] This possibility, this heavenly virtuality implicit in base matter, became a *credo*, an article of faith, for Gerard.

It was to become his life's blood and breath. Extraordinarily, during the scant two years remaining to him at St. Beuno's, he would write nearly one-third of his most renowned verse.

The authenticity, the authority, of his voice in the other great poems Gerard was to pen during his time there evokes the straight-forward and simple landscape of Wales. He rarely said something was "like" something else. He stretched for full and immediate presence. Gerard abolished analogy and dispensed with simile. In this, too, he followed Scotus. Scotus had mandated that "what is first known be attained perfectly, and this is so when it is attained in itself and not just in some diminished and derivative likeness of itself."[34] Gerard struggled, he wrestled, he grappled, and he re-fined until he could set down on paper, simply (although, many who read him would say, nevertheless exceedingly complexly), the word that spoke the essence of the creature into being. Scotus would have called this the creature's "thisness," its *haeccitas*. Arriv-ing at this knowledge of essence was, Scotus had said, "*intuitive*, like that of an angel." But Scotus had also spoken of the *artisanal* quality potential in human creation, suggesting that the difference between the divine Word and human word lay in that "our word is formable before it is formed":[35] hence Gerard's emphasis on technique and care and attentiveness.[36] Gerard felt he had found, and heard, the Word—God's Word, the idea in God's mind even before the creature was created. He "knew the who and the why; / Wording it how but by him that present and past, / Heaven and earth are word of, worded by."[37]

Scotus had explained how this relationship among man, na-ture, and God could occur. For Scotus, a reflective act (as con-trasted with a "direct act") is: "I want myself to know God, or: I know that I know God. In a reflective act a mediate object—

myself who wants, or the knowing 'I'—is inserted between the subject and the object of that act."[38] For Gerard, that "mediate object" was the natural world. For someone as interior and basically solitary as Gerard, books were presences as real as people, and poems were words spoken to and for and by him to a transcendent Other. Through his poetry, Gerard felt he became a participant in the creative work of God.

Such a notion of participation diverged from what Aquinas had taught concerning general and specific election. Aquinas had said that God alone determines, by assigning varying structures to creatures when he created them, what he will do with them. He does not consult them or require their assent. But for Scotus, who stressed love above all, and the inclusion of will to love, the creature in its unique particularity had the ability to respond to God, to co-respond. Gerard began to sense that aesthetics—the craft and cultivation of beauty—might be his own sort of loving responsiveness. Aesthetics might yield sanctity. If "every pure perfection is communicable,"[39] as Scotus had taught, then it should be communicated, Gerard reasoned. This was a reason to resume writing poetry. Poetry could not utterly contain the perfect, because the perfect always surpasses all other forms, but poetry could describe and exemplify the perfect and, in that way, in some measure point to, and participate in, what was perfect. Poetry might become a "sacramental." So, the nun was not Christ but could surpass herself and be *as* Christ; the windhover was not Christ, yet in its glorious freedom of *self as created*, it *figured forth* Christ, God's first "outstress," God's first act of love. Gerard was not Christ, yet in this newfound mediatory capacity ("the uniting medium," as Scotus called it, which "can be given the special name of reaching out and coming into contact with the other . . . or a stretching out and extending into the other")[40] of Gerard as priestly poet and intercessor, he could participate in the cosmic Christ, Christ in all creatures, shining out "as from shook foil." Gerard was not constructing an analogy; he was invoking a relationship.

Looking at his life in those days from the outside, in retrospect, we might say Gerard, though posted to many places, did
not have a very eventful life. However, his poetic experimentations *were* the events and experiences of his life, wrung from him
at times of high emotion—ecstasy, tragedy, devotion—wrestled
from his wordsmith's stock-in-trade, written into his relationship
with Christ. Gerard's theology shaped the framework, and his
aesthetic sensibility provided the form. The result was his true
self, spelled out on the page.

At St. Beuno's, during the summer of 1877, Gerard poured his
soul into his verses, crafting a constellation of remarkable poems.
Dovetailing his observations and insights, Gerard repurposed
some of his images from promptings of his prose: in his journal
for October 19, Gerard observed, "the clouds westwards were a
pied piece—sail-coloured brown and milky blue; a dun yellow
tent of rays opened upon the skyline far off. Cobalt blue was
poured on the hills."[41] "Pied Beauty" was a paean of praise to the
glory of God found in the Welsh countryside. Gerard told like
rosary beads his chance encounters during a summer stroll on a
sunny day: "Glory be to God for dappled things— / For skies of
couple-colour as a brinded cow; / For rose-moles all in stipple
upon trout that swim; / Fresh-firecoal chestnut-falls; finches'
wings; / Landscape plotted and pieced." The poem switches focus from earth to heaven, then back to earth. The oddities and
vagaries of nature, "All things counter, original, spáre, strange,"[42]
are the continued expressions of a perfect, and therefore unal-
tering, God, who nevertheless never ceases to create. Nature's
beauty, which Gerard viewed as the physical manifestation of
God's energy, produced a state of sanctification, an easing and a
self-acceptance within Gerard's soul, his secret, inner self phrased
into being, fused to verse. "Pied Beauty" is absolute in its acceptance of nature as a privileged medium of the revelation of
God, repeating the word "all" several times, and resolving apparent polarities in the clasp of paradox: God begins and ends the

poem, its Alpha and Omega, and all else held within that vast reach is known and loved by God. The poet's task and privilege was to witness all within that divine embrace. Gerard continued to communicate this intermingling of sacred and profane in his sermons, drawing on his poetry as a treasure trove for imagery and themes; on October 25, 1880, he rephrased the insights of "Pied Beauty" and its "landscape plotted and pieced," in this way: "search the whole world and you will find it a million-million fold contrivance of providence planned for our use and patterned for our admiration."[43]

In "Caged Lark," Gerard's soul was the lark. With a nostalgia for heaven, a belonging elsewhere, the poem recalls Wordsworth's "Intimations Ode" but is even stronger, yearning to extricate the soul from a material "prison" so that it may fly to its "own nest," as the soul will be homed to God in the resurrection, when it leaves its "bone-house" and, like a rainbow on "meadow-down," is transmuted into light, leaving earthly substance behind. Here, too, an experience of natural beauty led Gerard to an experience of sanctification and spiritual elevation.

The glad shout of "Hurrahing in Harvest" is like the trumpet blast that tumbled down Jericho's walls: an exuberant, even ecstatic, poem composed one hot afternoon in early September as Gerard was tramping the fields home after fishing for trout. Observing hay stooks in golden glory tossed all about him, from their beauty he "glean[ed]" Christ, harvesting him for his poem. "Hurrahing in Harvest" sees Christ as actually and fully present in the gleaming abundance of scythed grass ("Í lift úp heart, éyes / Down all that glory in the heavens to glean our Saviour"); in that way it is sacramental: "And the azurous hung hills are his world-wielding shoulder." It is a poem about immanence and the indwelling of the divine and the rare, mystic moments of utter joy when access is granted to this: "These things, these things were here and but the beholder / Wánting." Gerard looked at the landscape and venerated it, as though he were devoutly kneeling in church for the adoration of the Reserved Sacrament. The harvest was the Host. Gerard experienced a lifting, an elevation, almost a teleportation: "The heart rears wings bold and bolder / And hurls for him, O half hurls earth for him off under his feet."[44] The poet's role was to be, as a pun, "the beholder / Wánting": the necessary ("wanting") observer to these divine things revealed within materiality, and also the observer who deeply desires ("wanting") to see the God indwelling.

In "The Lantern out of Doors," Gerard wrote in implicit counterpoint to lines from the Gospel of John read liturgically for the Feast of the Epiphany and for Candlemas, feasts of light: "the light shines in the darkness, and the darkness has not comprehended it,"[45] as he sees that light which is in all men, and which darkness can neither suppress nor understand. Gerard described sitting at a window at night, glimpsing occasional lights twinkling off in the distance, knowing men were passing by. He marked their beauty and their life. Like the pink-patterned trout in "Pied Beauty," all humanity here is passing fair and strange: "Men go by me, whom either beauty bright / In mould or mind or what not else makes rare." All men, all creatures, have potential beauty, a light within by which they may be blessed. The eyes of the poet might lose sight of their inner light as they passed by him and faded into darkness, and, in fact, even as priest he admitted, once life cedes to death, "be in at the end / I cannot." Yet his task was, like that of the disciple John, to witness—his "I . . . eye[s]" them in love—and, in his poetry, to perpetuate them. And even so, these lights burn forever bright in the eyes of Christ: "Death or distance soon consumes them: wind, / What most I may eye after . . . / . . . and out of sight is out of mind. / Christ minds: Christ's interest, what to avow or amend / There, éyes them."[46]

Gerard's poetic epiphany was heady stuff. But he had not been sent to Wales to write poetry. He had been sent to study theology, usually a four-year endeavor. St. Beuno's was, in fact, a rigorous institution, and the rector, Father Gallwey, imposed many examinations and held to exacting standards. It was time to buckle down, time to study theology—more Ignatius and much less Scotus. Or less Suarez (a Jesuit neo-scholastic whom Gerard admired for his theology of the incarnation and of the Eucharist) and more neo-Thomism (since at least one of Gerard's chief examiners, Bernard Tepe, espoused the neo-Thomism of Leo XIII).[47] This was problematic for Gerard, who found it appealing that, unlike Aquinas, Scotus always spoke of theology as a *practical* science.

Theology was meant to be conducted by humans, and it was useful in leading human actions to their intended culmination in love for God. Scotus declared, "all things are a kind of intermediate for the object of reflective acts by means of which one tends to the infinite good, which is God." This notion of "intermediate" things could lead to Gerard's eventual understanding of his poetic act as a sort of "sacramental," as already discussed—for him as well as for others. What is ground for being, Scotus asserted, is also ground for knowing.[48] This view appealed to Gerard, with his elevated conception of poetry: poetry could be an action leading to divine love. Jesuitical casuistry, however, allowed for the possibility of negotiating salvation independent of the creature's love for God. For Scotus, and for Gerard, love was everything. Love was the reason for the incarnation, not sin. And love could be known intuitively, not syllogistically. Love could be known, grasped, enacted, *poetically*.

It was perhaps not a surprise, even to Gerard, that he performed poorly on his theology exam, though he did well on everything else. Whatever the case, he was ordained a priest shortly thereafter, in September 1877, but was not permitted to finish the customary fourth year of theology.[49] He and two other students who had not done well on theology exams were sent out to teach. Gerard's posting was to Mount St. Mary's (formerly the College of the Immaculate Conception), built by Hansom in 1840, located on land that had once belonged to Cardinal Reginald Pole's family, and site of some of the earliest and most ardent recusant activity in England. Near Chesterfield in the North Midlands, St. Mary's was a secondary institution of some 150 students, generally pupils whose families could not afford the high fees of a school like Stonyhurst. Gerard was given many teaching duties, including being master of boys aged eleven through thirteen. A disaster as a disciplinarian, Gerard nonetheless did love his pupils and was proud when a few of them won prizes.

But the nearest substantial town, Sheffield, depressed Gerard; it was smoky and unappealing, with muddy, rutted roads and gaping coal mines, a dark and terrible contrast to the verdant landscape of St. Beuno's. To bolster his spirits, Gerard wrote to Bridges frequently, and he sent to Dixon, now an Anglican vicar and a published poet, a new poem he called "Brothers." The subject had grown out of Gerard's work hearing schoolboy confessions and was his response to witnessing an act of compassion and altruism from one lad to another. Gerard was trying to find beauty around him in these everyday interactions, and to write into his poetry some of his experiences. With a good deal of fatigue and frustration in his daily grind, he tried to discern goodness all about, writing the poem almost as a parable, with its conclusion like a lullaby, its repeated refrain almost seeming to insist too much: "dearly thou canst be kind; / There dearly then, dearly, / Dearly thou canst be kind."[50]

But the psychic strain, and some physiological accompanying symptoms, told on him. On October 4, 1877, he requested to be circumcised. Was this neurosis? A rekindled obsession with purity? A visible sign that he alone construed as a reaffirmation of his consecration to God? The *Encyclopaedia Britannica*, published the year previous, although identifying religious motivations for circumcision among Jews, Muslims, and "tribal peoples," considered circumcision among contemporary Christians to be ritualistic self-mutilation, a "representative sacrifice."[51] The medical profession of Hopkins's day did perform this procedure (although customarily not after the age of three) to correct phimosis.[52] Scholars have analyzed the recourse, in cases like Gerard's, to surgery, deemed necessary by contemporary "medico-moral politics," to avoid perils such as masturbation. Regardless of the reason, the circumcision, no doubt painful and momentous for one reason or another, was performed.

Gerard again took up the themes of damage and despair. Gerard heard in March 1878 of the wreck of yet another ship, the *Eurydice*, and again decided to write about it. The poem expressed dark loss and dwelled on the beautiful physical lineaments, even in death, of the corpse of a sailor. His hands are gnarled from gripping ropes; his muscles are sturdy from working the rigging; and yet he is drowned, exhibited for veneration like a *pieta* as a woman weeps over him: "O well wept, mother have lost son." For the first time, Gerard seemed to question Christ ("wondering why my master bore it"), a rare and bitter moment perhaps indicating his own psychic distress at the time; while the sailor's body is comely, it is not, like that of the tall nun in the *Deutschland*, heroic. And yet, it is fitting—Gerard noted almost distractedly, "how all things suit"—this life, and this death, are what the sailor intended himself for, crafted himself for, sacrificed himself for: "Look, foot to forelock . . . he / Is strung by duty, is strained to beauty." In his fullest apprehension of the sense of the sailor's self, Gerard already begins to intuit a cosmic transformation: the corpse is returning to its natural components, "brine and shine and whirling wind." Perhaps Gerard understood his circumcision in this way: as a symbol, as an offering. And his poetic preservation of the *pieta* is akin to eternal prayer that holds the memory of "Life, this wildworth blown so sweet," this sad loss, yet not waste, of beautiful youth: "'And the prayer thou hearst me making / Have, at the awful overtaking, / Heard; have heard and granted / Grace that day grace was wanted.'"[53] Loss of life leads to resurrection in memory; beauty, whether in life or in death, is hallowed. Still, a melancholic mood overlies this poem. This was a new note for Gerard, not one of unadulterated exultation but a sound of sad resignation, a chord that would increasingly prevail in his later poetry.

Briefly sent back to Stonyhurst from April to July of 1878 to prepare students for examinations in classics, Gerard reverted to his earlier lightheartedness for a time. Commissioned to write a poem to grace the statue of the Blessed Mother on May Day, he responded with the lilting "May Magnificat," which, probably because of its sprung rhythm like a dance or jig of joy, the Jesuits deemed too larking and lively to be used. In this sweet meditation on how it must have been for Mary to bear within her God's very self, Gerard pondered the purpose of all created things and stored up their sense in his heart: "This ecstasy all through mothering earth / Tells Mary her mirth till Christ's birth / To remember and exultation / In God who was her salvation." Gerard made himself like Mary; his mothering was his versing. Mary promotes "Growth in everything— / Flesh and fleece, fur and feather, / Grass and greenworld all together." Her burgeoning, and the growing to fullness of the month of May, births the cosmic Christ: "With delight calls to mind / How she did in her stored / Magnify the Lord." Mary is "mighty," fecund with "that world of good, / Nature's motherhood." Each creature is individually distinct and also related "in its kind," as Gerard recalled Scotus's teaching of the particularity of worth. Mary's mothering affirms "all things rising, all things sizing." Her impregnation by the Holy Spirit is distilled beautifully from dogma down to natural reality in Gerard's image of the cuckoo ("And magic cuckoocall / Caps, clears, and clinches all"):[54] the cuckoo, a bird that nests in others' nests, as Christ was enwombed by divine agency yet housed by a human father. Heaven and earth conjoin in this way, as the explosion of new birth and beauty in May reenact the incarnation.

But the emotional ease Gerard may have felt at Stonyhurst was short-lived, and he continued to struggle. His preaching was not well received; invited by his former novice master Father Gallwey, now pastor at the toney Jesuit Church of the Immaculate

Conception on Farm Street in London, Gerard thoroughly scandalized the society matrons in attendance by creatively comparing the gracious availability of the seven sacraments of the church to milk flowing from the teats of a cow's udder![55]

By November 1878, his Jesuit superiors, at a loss what to do with the brilliant but increasingly odd and reclusive priest, sent Gerard back to Oxford. He was to function as curate of St. Aloysius, a rather nondescript structure, enlivened within by a smattering of Pre-Raphaelite stained glass windows, erected on a slice of land Newman had purchased years earlier, intending it for the establishment of the Oxford Oratory. Gerard had not set foot in Oxford for over a decade, and he was shy of renewing former acquaintances and concerned that past episodes of undergraduate high spirits might tarnish his priestly image. He stuck to his charitable and social work and served diligently as associate curate, though he tired easily and complained of spiritual aridity.[56] Gerard saw Walter Pater a few times and sometimes dined with a hospitable Roman Catholic family with whom he was to maintain close contact for the rest of his life, the Paravicinis, whom he knew through Balliol College connections,[57] but mostly he kept to himself.

He also found Protestant opposition to any Catholic presence at Oxford unabated. High Church Anglicanism, with ever more elaborate liturgy and ornate organ recitals, continued to flourish. The Anglican church of St. Barnabas filled all 1,200 seats in its pews every Sunday, making it difficult for Gerard to obtain the middle-class conversions the Society of Jesus hoped for. At the same time, local working-class folk, many of them Irish Catholic immigrants, tended to view Oxford Movement converts such as Gerard with suspicion, considering them uppity interlopers into the Catholic fold; some even refused to receive Holy Communion at his hands, further discouraging Gerard.[58] Gerard was not an ideal clergyman to minister to working-class folk, anyway; his flamboyant affectations, such as waving a bright red handkerchief to emphasize whatever he was saying, were seen as suspect. Many parishioners were unhesitatingly and distressingly vocal in their criticisms of church services. Gerard wrote to Bridges, "they had not as a body the charming and cheering heartiness of those Lancashire Catholics, which is so deeply comforting."[59] But Gerard did his best. He visited the sick, heard confessions, administered extreme unction and last rites for the dying, catechized, baptized, married, and buried. He was very busy, very obedient to the expectations of his superiors. When he could wrest a moment from his pastoral rounds, he scrawled notes and fragments of verse on the back of mass cards or on fliers soliciting funds for the altar-guild needleworkers of St. Aloysius.

While at Oxford, Gerard corresponded extensively with Bridges, although they continued to fence with each other over their differing religious beliefs; he continued his correspondence with Dixon as well. Gerard's poetry from this period seems more socially engaged than other of his poems: in "Binsey Poplars," he reacted as something of a proto-environmentalist to the clear-cutting of poplars along the Thames, and he wrote poetry about the nearby military barracks for which he was the soldiers' curate. "Binsey Poplars" clearly displayed Gerard's Scotist inclination to regard elements of nature as personages, distinct and particular in their essences, worthy of consideration; just as to people, violence can "unselve" them. He called the trees "my aspens dear" and described the countryside as a delicate maiden ("Since country is so tender / To tóuch, her béing só slénder"); thus, to deprive the world of the power and presence of trees was tantamount to a rape ("if we but knew what we do / When we delve or hew— / Hack and rack the growing green!"). Once the landscape is violated, "after-comers cannot guess the beauty been," but Gerard's verse resurrects, perpetuates that lost and fallen beauty. The poet is a priest, an intercessor, an intermediary, an interpreter of "The sweet especial scene, / Rural scene, a rural scene, / Sweet especial rural scene."[60]

While he was at Oxford and while in London, Gerard indulged in the other sort of experience that characterized his solitary, cerebral life: he went to museums and art galleries, listened to music, particularly that of Dvořák and Purcell, whom he adulated and called "so arch especial a spirit,"[61] read Dickens and Stevenson and Shakespeare. He also read Tennyson, whom he treated dismissively as inadequate to the present day, or at least not up to Gerard's self-imposed poetical standards: "the poetical language of an age shd. be the current language heightened, to any degree heightened and unlike itself, but not . . . an obsolete one. This is Shakespeare's and Milton's practice and the want of it will be fatal to Tennyson."[62] Gerard was populating his internal mental universe, trying to fix on an alternative reality to blot out the discouraging drab drone of cities. His spirituality, always aesthetic, lent itself well to such shaping and refining. He was also trying to bolster the strength of his vocation by eschewing ugliness and vulgarity, press and noise and strife. He confessed to Dixon, "A purpose may look smooth and perfect from without but be frayed and faltering from within. I have never wavered in my vocation, but I have not lived up to it."[63]

Gerard was discouraged by the transformation of Oxford since his time there. The town was becoming industrialized, and Gerard never did well in manufacturing cities, where poverty and misery were so much in evidence and the clatter of machinery shouted down birdsong. From October to December of 1879, the Society of Jesus deployed Gerard as supply clergy to St. Joseph's, Bedford Leigh, near Manchester, another dank industrial town. Numerous collieries pocked the outlying countryside, and after 1858, when a private railway line had linked the depots in order to transport coal more efficiently, the formerly rural area became predominantly industrial. Nearby Manchester had experienced recent unprecedented growth due to its flourishing textile factories, and in 1853 for this reason had become the first English city to be designated in over three hundred years. Lacking any strategy for urban planning, the city loomed dirty and disorderly.

Gerard called Leigh a "darksome place," but he felt "far more at home" there with the denizens of Lancashire than he had in Oxford.[64] The population of Bedford Leigh was at least a quarter Roman Catholic, so it was easier to insinuate himself into life there. Leigh was a former center of secret recusant activity by several Roman Catholic families fervent to preserve the "old faith" during the Reformation. St. Joseph's Church was built by Joseph Hansom in 1855 on Chapel Street, on the site of a chapel erected in 1778 and subsequently destroyed. A brick structure in the Gothic Revival style, St. Joseph's distinctive slate roof featured dramatic fish-scale bands, and its interior was broad and open, with a strikingly large preaching box. From this spacious pulpit, Gerard preached most Sundays to a nearly full church. Perhaps because he felt more relaxed, his preaching style became simpler and more engaging, with reference to popular piety, legends, and miracles.

He began to write an ambitious, never-finished, verse drama entitled "The Tragedy of St. Winefred."[65] St. Winefred, niece of St. Beuno, was martyred in Wales in 660 when she spurned a man's advances. Where her beheaded body fell to the ground, a well sprang up. Another version of her legend recounts that St. Beuno replaced her head on her body, thereby resuscitating her, and she became the beloved abbess of a nearby convent. Her well, Holywell, was one of the most popular pilgrimage sites in Great Britain. Gerard's journal, and his interest in writing this drama, attested to his own lifelong faith in miraculous occurrences: "a young man . . . was cured of rupture [hernia] in the water. The strong unfailing flow of the water and the chain of cures from year to year all these centuries took hold of my mind with wonder at the bounty of God in one of His saints, the sensible thing so naturally and gracefully uttering the spiritual reason of its being (which is all in true keeping with the story of St. Winefred's death and recovery)." Crafting this verse drama was also a way to keep Wales, where he had bathed in the waters of Holywell "very joyously," ever present in his heart: "even now the stress and buoyancy and abundance of the water is before my eyes."[66]

Unlike the shift toward accessibility in his sermons, Gerard's verse continued to be unusual, difficult sometimes to understand, demanding much of the reader. Gerard wrote, "No doubt my poetry errs on the side of oddness.... Now it is the virtue of design, pattern, or inscape to be distinctive and it is the vice of distinctiveness to become queer."[67] He was equating his poetry with his own personality; his verse was his inscape; to read him was—if the reader could prevail over complexity—to know him.

Well-intentioned and admiring Dixon continued to read and to praise Gerard's work. He wrote that Gerard's poems were "among the most extraordinary I have ever read, amazingly original."[68] Dixon (1833–1900), friend of Edward Burne-Jones and William Morris at Exeter, had been Gerard's schoolmaster at Highgate School in London and was, further, an accomplished poet who was nominated for poet laureate after Tennyson's death. Winner of the Oxford Sacred Poem prize in 1863 for a composition about Saint John in the book of Revelation, Dixon had written early verses characterized by the color, flash, and determined flouting of tradition of some Pre-Raphaelite painting, with which many affiliated his verses stylistically.[69] Attentive to poetic experimentation and a firm believer that through poetry and other artistic endeavors one could accomplish great things for humanity, as long as one followed one's own inclinations and temperament, Dixon had compared Hopkins with Walt Whitman, of whom Gerard had written: "I always knew in my heart Walt Whitman's mind to be more like my own than any other man's living. As he is a very great scoundrel this is not a pleasant confession. And this also makes me the more desirous to read him and the more determined that I will not."[70]

In October, Dixon sent Gerard's poem "The Loss of the *Eurydice*" to a publisher without first asking Gerard's approval. Fearing censure from the Society of Jesus, from which permission should first have been requested, Gerard vehemently told Dixon that he did not want the poem published. More and more retiring and punctilious in his personal habits, Gerard feared the poem was inadequate and also that it would reflect badly on him: "what is not near enough for public fame may be more than enough for private notoriety, which is what I dread."[71]

All his friends, not just Dixon, were frustrated. They, and Gerard, spent an enormous amount of time conferring through correspondence in a sort of virtual literary circle, discussing each other's drafts, offering suggestions, changing a word here and there. What was the point, they wondered, if his poetry would never appear in print? But Gerard knew. He was writing for, and to, Christ. It was for Christ to determine how, and if ever, this poetry, these sacred love letters, would be used. On the three hundredth anniversary of the martyrdom of Edmund Campion, SJ, a telling choice of date on which to write his justification of his refusal to publish, Gerard wrote to Dixon,

> If I wait for [the guidance of my superiors or divine guidance] about my poetry . . . , I do more wisely in every way than if I try to serve my own seeming interests in the matter. Now if you value what I write, if I do myself, much more does our Lord. And if he chooses to avail himself of what I leave at his disposal he can do so with a felicity and with a success which I could never command. And if he does not, then two things follow; one that the reward I shall nevertheless receive from him will be all the greater; the other that then I shall know how much a thing contrary to his will and even to my own best interests I should have done if I had taken matters into my own hands and forced on publication.[72]

Gerard conceived of his life as material for Christ to craft with; he placed himself utterly at Christ's disposal.

Meanwhile, Gerard was to serve in yet another industrial city, this time Liverpool, to which he was sent in January 1880. The Jesuits filled a need at the parish of St. Francis Xavier in Liverpool, one of the largest Roman Catholic churches in England, built in 1842 by John Scoles and adorned with a white marble altar and reredos. His superiors designated Gerard one of nine vastly overworked pastors to a parish population of over ten thousand. Liverpool's population was over one-third Irish by this time, most of them immigrants and many unemployed shipbuilders, a formerly steady trade that had been undermined by the recent vogue for iron ships as well as by the need to expand the docks to accommodate more trade, which unsettled and disorganized the shipbuilders' unions. By 1880, the unemployment rate in Liverpool was the highest in Great Britain. Circumstances in Liverpool were dirty, degrading, and depressing.[73] Gerard witnessed poverty greater than he had ever seen before. The Irish were illiterate, ill-fed, poorly housed, and often drunk. Gerard, utterly discouraged, "so fagged, so harried and gallied," railed: "And the drunkards go on drinking, the filthy, as the scripture says, are filthy still."[74]

Gerard was also subjected to scrutiny by the other parish priests and required to submit his sermons for their revision (he was upbraided for using the suspect term "sweetheart" to describe Christ in one of his homilies).[75] Under stress, he began to lose control of his emotions; more than one parishioner commented that "little Father Hopkins had a little bit of a temper!"[76] Gerard struggled to write poetry, though the elegiac "Felix Randal" was written there. "Felix Randal" was a farrier and parishioner who had passed away subsequent to Gerard's anointing him. Gerard mourned his loss but used the poem as a medium through which to continue a relationship with the dead man; although the parochial interaction had been brought to an end: "is he déad then? my dúty all énded," the relationship of love and trust that grew through the pastoral interaction continued. "This séeing the síck endéars them tó us, us tóo it endéars. / My tongue had taught thee comfort, touch had quenched thy tears, / Thy tears that touched my heart, child, Felix, poor Felix Randal." The dead man's regional dialect permeated the poem, as Gerard imitates it, incorporating the speech patterns of the man he renamed "Felix" into the poem that memorialized him: "Áh well, God rést him áll road éver he offénded!" The unaccustomed intimate tone of sweet sorrow and mourning attested to Gerard's involvement with his flock and to the tenderness of his heart. The selection of a farrier, a rural worker who "fettle[d] for the great grey dray-horse,"[77] as subject of the sonnet also showed Gerard's loneliness and alienation from most of the urban area in which he served. He wrote, "Liverpool is of all places the most museless. It is indeed a most unhappy and miserable spot. There is moreover no time for writing anything serious."[78]

Nonetheless, Gerard did compose the evocative, mournful "Spring and Fall" while on a weekend visit to Lydiate in his beloved Lancashire, seeking surcease from his Liverpool tenure. Dated September 7, 1880, the poem aptly muses on the season of autumn but also reads it theologically as the fall of man from the spring of innocence. Opening and closing with the address to a "Young Child" named Margaret, the poem addresses a specific young girl whose insights, and fate, are those of humanity in general, as the poem moves from the particular to the universal in a Scotist manner. The child regrets the "unleaving" of a beautiful, fictive or mythic, place Gerard calls Goldengrove. The elision of the two words makes the place doubly Edenic: it is not just a grove that is golden, it is a grove that is the quintessence of goldenness. It is Paradise. Margaret watches its dismantlement, its "unleaving," and grieves, as new Eve cast out of the garden. Or her awareness may simply represent her impending adulthood. Whatever the case, the reader suspects that Margaret and Gerard are one and the same, as Gerard mourned lost days of rural beauty and bliss amid the crass clutch and constraint of city life. Margaret is grieving in the fall, as Goldengrove is "unleaving." The melancholy falling of the leaves sketches the downward descent of heart, and the theological Fall from grace: "It is the blight man was born for." The poem tries to comfort her, suggesting that Margaret, as she ages, may become inured to the loss of beauty: "Ah! as the heart grows older / It will come to such sights colder / By and by, nor spare a sigh / Though worlds of wanwood leafmeal lie." But such cold disenchantment would be a loss ("come to such sights colder"), and also, such a detachment will not happen: "And yet you *will* weep and know why," presumably because the fruit of the tree of knowledge has been eaten, and sorrow is the result. Though humanity cannot fathom its plight, the Holy Ghost intuits: "Nor mouth had, no nor mind, expressed / What heart heard of, ghóst guéssed"; watching the undoing of Goldengrove, the withdrawal of Paradise, entails a loss of self: "It is Margaret you mourn for."[79] This is consistent with Gerard's theology—all along he had insisted that one's true self was known in, and held by, God. But here, the note of loss, without any palliating comfort, is disturbing. Gerard, like Margaret, was mourning a lost self. He felt he was falling, falling out of relationship with Christ. And he had to return to Liverpool.

To divert himself from stretches of poetic unproductivity, Gerard turned again to music, penning a couple of original musical compositions. Fortunately, Gerard had to endure a stint of only twenty months in Liverpool. But the next posting was also industrial. He was dispatched to Glasgow, as assistant at St. Joseph's parish, a large urban church of some 1,200 pew seats off of Manresa Place. Glasgow was no improvement: "wretched place too Glasgow is, like all our great towns."[80] A city in decline due to a slack-off in shipbuilding, its forges and foundries less busy than before, Glasgow's many pubs were overfrequented, and its political situation was increasingly unsettled, with Irish Home Rule riots taking place.[81] The plight of the poor was horrific, with cholera and typhoid fever regularly decimating hordes housed in the putrid slums called "backlands."[82] Gerard anguished, "my

Liverpool and Glasgow experience laid upon my mind a conviction, a truly crushing conviction, of the misery of town life to the
poor . . . of the degradation even of our race, of the hollowness
of this century's civilization: it made even life a burden to me to
have daily thrust upon me the things I saw."[83] Like Ruskin and
many others in late Victorian England, Gerard was turning away
from the present day; his ritualism recalled medieval England;
his hero worship in his poetry evoked King Arthur's knights;
and his increasing solitariness and reclusiveness reinforced his
disillusionment. To make matters worse, Gerard's favorite correspondent, Bridges, was quite ill with pneumonia, and Gerard
missed his epistolary encouragement. He cringed, physically and
psychically, from the filth and fetid air of the cities.

Gerard was able to extricate himself from duties for a few days'
holiday in the Highlands, reveling in the pure air and unsullied
natural surroundings. At Loch Lomond, he wrote a first draft of
the poem "Inversnaid," celebrating this freedom and joy in nature.
Yet there was a dark undercurrent to the poem; he wrote it on an
overcast day, feeling somewhat melancholic, and the mood drags
the movement of the verses down, just as the river flows "low to
the lake" and "falls home," and "rounds and rounds Despair to
drowning." Gerard spoke of a particular river near Loch Lomond,
"this dárksome búrn, hórseback brówn, / His rollrock highroad
roaring down," observing it with Ruskinesque precision and minute scrutiny. At the end of the poem he moved from the specific
to the generalizable, documenting the loss of so much of nature
and wildness already by asking, "What would the world be, once
bereft / Of wet and of wildness? Let them be left, / O let them
be left."[84] Gerard, back in Glasgow, already knew the loss "of wet
and of wildness"; it was too late to implore, "O let them be left."
There are two characters in the poem: the river and Despair.

Gerard rarely capitalized nouns, but he capitalized "Despair,"
introducing a new, and deeply troubling, protagonist to his poetic universe. Despair swirls round in the vortex of the water,

producing a feeling of drowning, and Gerard had struggled with this element before, in both of his shipwreck poems. Yet he had found a sense for the sacrifice in "The Wreck of the *Deutschland*," and he had portrayed the fittingness of the sailor's end on the ship *Eurydice*. Drowning in "Inversnaid" was more ambiguous, more menacing. Seeking solace from the despair he felt in cities, Gerard was drawn to death. The poem offers no Christ as consoler; it dwells in a pantheist environment, at best. Perhaps only the rhetorical plea, "O let them be left," an exiguous prayer, suggests the continued presence of a divine interlocutor.

More and more Gerard felt himself psychically drawn down, worn out by work, failing to find sources of beauty to gladden his eye and heart. Reading Robert Louis Stevenson sometime later, he found a form for the darkness he increasingly experienced: he wrote to Bridges asking why some criticized Stevenson's Mr. Hyde as an exaggeration; "my Hyde," Gerard wrote, in a rare moment of self-disclosure, "is worse."[85]

After assisting at St. Joseph's in Glasgow, Gerard was sent back to Manresa. There, he and all the other priests in their third and final year as novices made the Long Retreat again. The aim was to recover the fervor that had initially impelled their decision to accept the vocation of Jesuit. Gerard enjoyed the respite from the cities; he relaxed, reflected, and wrote to Bridges, "my mind is here more at peace than it has ever been and I would gladly live all my life . . . in as great or a greater seclusion from the world and be busied only with God."[86] His increasingly doubled, divided, self, that dark dog Hyde, did not make an appearance at Manresa.

On August 16, 1882, the Feast of the Assumption, Gerard was formally professed spiritual coadjutor. Spiritual coadjutors are priests who make the traditional three vows of poverty, chastity, and obedience. This is a full final ordination but with limits: only priests permitted to make the fourth vow, distinct to the Society of Jesus, of particular obedience to the pope are thereby enabled to advance to positions as superiors, novice masters, and other higher ranks in the Society. Because Gerard had not done well in theology, he was not permitted to make the fourth vow. Henceforth, he would live in community, continue to serve where he was sent, and be occupied primarily with teaching.[87] While Gerard had known of the itinerant nature of many Jesuits, he had not fully taken it into consideration in the early days of his enthusiasm, focusing more on the constant dedication to God and the spiritual discipline that the Jesuits provided. The realization that he had already undergone many postings, and would have many more to endure, exhausted him emotionally and spiritually. He was next sent to teach Latin, Greek, and English literature to Catholic students at Stonyhurst in London. Gerard felt isolated there, on the margins, socially excluded, and unable to write poetry. He confided plaintively, tellingly, to Bridges, "I seem but half a man,"[88] adding, "I have been in a wretched state of weakness and weariness, I can't tell why, always drowzy and incapable of reading or thinking to any effect."[89]

However, some relief and distraction came through a new acquaintance: the noted poet, novelist, and mystic Coventry Patmore, invited to do the graduation speech at Stonyhurst in 1883. Coventry Kersey Dighton Patmore (1823–1896) was at the time best known for a lengthy poem in narrative form inspired by his first wife, Emily. Entitled "The Angel in the House" (1855–1862), the poem argued for recognition of the poet, Patmore himself, as possessing superior spiritual insight and the ability to discern how the language of erotic and conjugal love both paralleled and led to an awareness of the divine love relationship between God and the soul. Although comparisons have been drawn to the love imagery of Saint John of the Cross, not everyone was persuaded.[90] The poem also put forward a very Victorian ideal of domestic female perfection. (Gerard expressed himself equivocally on the subject, saying daintily, he "does not seem to me quite to hit the mark in this profoundly delicate matter.")[91]

Patmore had also penned some art criticism, having been close friends with Dante Gabriel Rossetti and been part of the Pre-Raphaelite coterie in his younger days as a prize-winning painter as well as poet. Patmore had become a Roman Catholic very shortly after the lingering death of his wife in 1862. He remarried and in 1877 produced an acclaimed poem, "The Unknown Eros." He was a great admirer of Tennyson, the poet laureate. Like Gerard, Patmore was a perfectionist and somewhat of a poetic minimalist: in a collected edition of his works published in 1886, Patmore's preface stated, "I have written little, but it is all my best."

Gerard admired Patmore's poetry and shared some of his own verse with him. Patmore, who knew Bridges, wrote him that Gerard's poetry "has the effect of veins of pure gold imbedded in masses of unpracticable quartz,"[92] suggesting the beauty and brilliance of Gerard's insights but also acknowledging the complex, balky syntax in which he phrased them. It is true that Gerard increasingly found himself on the defensive with his coterie of friendly critics; his imagery was unusual, microscopically specific ("and this is true of nothing else"), intensely personal ("not the same as yours"), not easily communicated ("no other word whatever will give the effect I want") in its evocation and expression, its syntax challenging to understand. Bridges, in possession of fair copies of most of Gerard's poems, was contemplating an edition of them, and asked for clarification, among others, of the image of "shook foil" that Gerard had developed in "God's Grandeur," and the explanation, while ultimately compelling, was lengthy and complicated: "But the image is not the same as yours and I do not mean by foil set-off at all; I mean foil in its sense of leaf or tinsel, and no other word whatever will give the effect I want. Shaken goldfoil gives off broad glares like sheet lightning and also, and this is true of nothing else, owing to its zigzag dints and creasings and network of small many cornered facets, a sort of fork lightning too."[93] The only way to understand what Gerard was saying was to become Gerard, to see through his eyes. While Patmore and Gerard continued to correspond, they never became close friends, always addressing each other formally, "my dear sir."

Meanwhile, Gerard's superiors put him forward for the position of professor of Greek recently opened at University College, Dublin, Ireland. Their recommendation was qualified, at best. They recognized Gerard's eccentricities: his tendency to over-commit himself and fall ill or prey to exhaustion or depression; his struggles with excessive scrupulosity; his limitations within the Society of Jesus. But they also knew something had to be done with him, and they knew he was a brilliant scholar. Father Delaney, who had lobbied for the establishment of a Catholic college whose graduates would be able to rival those of the Anglican Trinity College, had overseen as president the college's move on November 12, 1883, into the buildings of Newman's Catholic University, founded in 1850. Father Delaney sought well-qualified professors with solid academic expertise from an international pool of possibilities. Despite Irish opposition to the appointment of an English Jesuit, and despite some reservations concerning Gerard's lack of publications in the field, in January 1884 Gerard was elected to the faculty of University College, Dublin, in the Department of Classics. He moved to Dublin on February 18, 1884. There, Gerard was also given the responsibility of administering and grading university examinations, which were legion. For Gerard, plagued by a compulsion to perfectionism, this would be the beginning of his end. He lamented to Bridges, "It is an honour ... and has many bright sides, but at present it has also some dark ones and this in particular that I am not at all strong," and he said, "Dublin ... is a joyless place."[94]

Chapter 4   DESOLATION

As kingfishers catch fire, dragonflies draw flame;
     As tumbled over rim in roundy wells
        Stones ring; like each tucked string tells, each
            hung bell's
     Bow swung finds tongue to fling out broad
          its name;
     Each mortal thing does one thing and the same:
        Deals out that being indoors each one dwells;
        Selves—goes its self; myself it speaks and spells,
     Crying What I do is me: for that I came.[1]

IN DUBLIN, GERARD'S psyche and his soul, his sense of duty and his sense of loss, his lack of strength, his feeling of being an outsider and a stranger among the Irish all pressured him in unbearable ways. His sense of "being indoors each one dwells; / Selves" felt confused and lost and strange. In this dark, windy, remorselessly gray city, Gerard no longer felt hope or purpose other than that "great system and machinery which even drags me on with the collar round my neck . . . [and] I am not willing enough for the piece of work assigned me, the only work I am given to do," he confessed.[2] He was to spend five years in Dublin; it was to be the longest single posting of his life as a Jesuit, and virtually every day brought more despondency. Dublin was charcoal dark; its air was filled with soot. There was pervasive poverty, and the urban areas and nearby outlying areas were crammed with indigents suffering from malnutrition and illness.[3] Gerard, too, having always been in fragile health, began to break down.

The character of Despair, who had made its appearance in the poem "Inversnaid," now became a familiar, and other protagonists emerged to play parts in the drama, a spiritual tragedy, that had become Gerard's life. Among them were Patience—sorely lacking; Time—inadequate and unavailing, yet also dragging and slow; Darkness—lacking a light; Hell—conspiring with "dark Heaven" to deny Gerard; God—become a mad wrestler and inflictor of suffering; Death—now desired; and Gerard himself, whom he at least three times deemed "a eunuch," a divided, self-loathing, sin-tasting self disunited from his soul. Christ the hero, and the self who could conjoin with Christ through contemplation of the glories of God in the world, was a dim memory.

Gerard wrote incessantly to Bridges of this cast of characters. In letter after letter he castigated himself for not being able to do anything beyond the dull dead grind of grading examinations, sacrificing all his energies to thankless administrative tasks. He began to envision publication, the production of a book of poetry, only to realize that his labors to produce were in vain, a "straining" like a woman in false labor. He said, "All my undertakings miscarry: I am like a straining eunuch. I wish then for death."[4] He spoke of their group of friends, fellow poets and correspondents, and wistfully admired what others had accomplished, seeming to reverse himself on his earlier resolution to leave it to Christ to decide what posterity might make of his poetry, if anything. But he realized, "Our society cannot be blamed for not valuing what it never knew of. [My poems] are therefore, one may say, unknown. . . . I have long been at a standstill, and so the things lie."[5] Dublin became his Golgotha, where Gerard hung himself on the cross of his own failed endeavors, and mocked and spurned himself, drinking vinegar, not wine.

He had thought, for once, to refuse his superiors' orders; he had hoped not to go to Dublin. But he had taken vows of obedience. When he arrived in Dublin on February 18, 1884, he found a college in disarray, a few of its buildings in rubble, most dilapidated, an utterly inadequate and unsanitary plumbing system, pervading cold and damp. The college "is a sort of ruin and for purposes of study very nearly naked," Gerard wrote to Bridges.[6]

Appointed a fellow of the Royal University of Ireland in Dublin, Gerard was one of several examiners who received a small salary that helped offset the expenses of University College, where he was not to begin teaching until the fall of 1884. At the Royal University of Ireland, Gerard was expected to grade six examinations yearly, and he painstakingly marked papers late into the night, repeatedly going back over their scoring to be sure of its accuracy and fairness, his head aching and a stabbing pain in his eyes. While others might have compromised or taken their task less seriously, Gerard's scrupulousness made that impossible. He wrapped his head in a wet towel and slogged on with the thankless task.

These examinations were not only necessary to attest to the students' progress within the university; they were also vital in publicizing the worth and caliber of the newly formed university in contrast to other, nonsectarian or Protestant universities throughout Ireland. Students must perform well; their prizes and attainments, after being excruciatingly calibrated and documented by Gerard, would then attest to the very high and exacting standards of the Catholic educational system.

The following year, he was informed, he would also be expected to lecture. Jesuits return all their salary to the Society, so Gerard's 400 pounds per annum was sent back to help develop the university, but he quickly came to feel that the university was a problematic venture as well as counterproductive to his desire to create: "soon I am afraid I shall be ground down to a state [as before], when my spirits were so crushed that madness seemed to be making approaches."[7] His always chronic anxiety became overwhelming. He was "thought by most to be more or less crazy. There was something unusual about him. He was fond of pursuing niceties to an extent that stood in the way of his usefulness," fellow faculty members observed.[8] A new faculty member in an aspirationally rigorous institution, Gerard was further frustrated by the need he felt to write academic studies in order to measure up to scholarly norms. He drafted essays on Sophocles and Pindar, and some speculative pieces on the nature of light, the composition of the atmosphere, and statistics, but none of these was accepted for publication. He was only able to publish a few songs taken from Shakespeare that Gerard had translated into Latin. He came to believe that, as he said to Bridges, nothing "of mine will ever see the light—of publicity nor even of day. . . . The mortification that goes to the heart is to feel it is the power that fails you. . . . If I could but get on, if I could but produce work I should not mind its being buried, silenced, and going no further; but it kills me to be time's eunuch and never to beget."[9]

He was also troubled by the times; riots for Home Rule occurred frequently, tempers flared and the suffering of the Irish could not be denied: visible evidence of it confronted him every day. Landlords had become so extortionate that families were evicted, unable to pay their rent, and lived in holes dug into the ground then covered with straw. Entire families huddled below ground, without daylight, like a living burial. Charles Stewart Parnell was at the peak of his popularity, and negotiating in Parliament, with some apparent success, to obtain a separate parliament for Ireland while keeping Ireland in the British Empire, even persuading Prime Minister Gladstone by 1885 of the need for Home Rule.[10] Nonetheless, conditions in Ireland were so untenable that a vigilante group named Captain Moonlight, agrarian rebels representing the radical Land League, took matters into their own hands, threatening landlords with torture or death—at first symbolically, burning in effigy, maiming cattle, setting fire to hayricks. A scant few years before Gerard's arrival, on May 6, 1882, Lord Frederick Cavendish, viceroy of Ireland, and his undersecretary had both been stabbed to death while strolling in Phoenix Park by an Irish murder gang, self-styled "the Invincibles," patriots for Irish freedom. Bombs were set off in Glasgow and Ireland in 1883; in 1884 there was a terrorist attempt to blow up London Bridge.[11] The situation was dire, and the stakes were high for England: in the heyday of empire, if England were not able to govern Ireland, a part of Great Britain, how would England govern the far-flung colonies, impose order in India, and dominate African trade. *Habeas corpus* had been suspended in Ireland; imprisonments without warrant were routine.

Despite his innate loyalty to England, Gerard was drawn to the political stance of William Morris, the founding father of British socialism.[12] Gerard admired his activism, along with that of Annie Besant, three of whose socialist lectures he attended in Ireland,[13] and that of Beatrice Webb, a leading Fabian socialist.[14] Gerard commiserated over the plight of the poor in Ireland, both in countryside and in city. Further, he believed that change was both necessary and inevitable; the Irish simply would not cooperate with the English government. "England is most perilously hated" over here, he wrote to Bridges.[15]

There had been a huge "Irish row" over Gerard being admitted as the sole Englishman to the university, and this was merely a small symptom of the tension and hostilities prevailing in Ireland. Gerard felt the Irish were basically ungovernable, acknowledging no principle of civil law and resorting to violence and illegal acts to achieve their goals. Yet he also sympathized; he had arrived in Dublin a homesick Englishman, but he quickly became critical of the brutal English policy toward the Irish. "It has always been the fault of the mass of Englishman to know and care nothing about Ireland, to let be what would there (which, as it happened, was persecution, avarice, and oppression)." To Bridges, he wrote, "it is the beginning of the end: Home Rule or separation is near. Let them come. . . . I shd. be glad to see Ireland happy, even though it involved the fall of England." But Gerard held out no hopes for a radical improvement, even so; all was despair and hopelessness: "distress will bring on some fresh convulsion."[16]

These dire straits of the Home Rule agitations depressed Gerard even further. Fairly early during his time in Dublin, probably during his first year there, Gerard drafted the poem "The Times Are Nightfall." He revised the poem again in 1885 or 1886. It proved prophetic of the physical exhaustion he was experiencing and also of the spiritual trials besetting him. The poem makes observations, just as Gerard had been taught to do by Ruskin and Pater, and as he had done in the past when documenting nature's beauty and perceiving God therein. After each observation, the poem expresses an imperative; it orders the poet to use his eyesight, both physical and inner sight, to discern the meaning of what he observes: "The times are nightfall, look, their light grows less; / The times are winter, watch, a world undone." But the technique he had always relied on no longer functioned; he was unable to see, to understand. All was darkness. "The times are nightfall." The Light, the Logos, no longer shines in the darkness ("nor word now"), as it did in the Gospel of John, and as it had for Gerard, Christ present in the world. Not in his world anymore. Not in Gerard's dreary life in Dublin. And he saw no remedy: "And I not help." The phrase is ambiguous. Did he receive no help from Christ? Did Gerard mean that he conspired against himself? Did his depression undo him, make of him "a world undone"? The poem is filled with words beginning in *w*: "winter," "waste," "wither," "wreck," and even "work," effort expiring in wind and feeble whistle, suggesting that Gerard's endeavors, his poetic work, that which he felt he had to offer of beauty and significance to God, was not acceptable: "Nor word now of success: / All is from wreck, here, there, to rescue one— / Work which to see scarce so much as begun / Makes welcome death." Again, the face of Death appears. The final three lines of the poem might offer comfort, might suggest a way forward, an alternative to this bleak, unrelenting suffering and impotence: "Or what is else? There is your world within. / There rid the dragons, root out there the sin. / Your will is law in that small commonweal."[17]

Gerard's inner self might then be compared to Ireland ("that small commonweal") misgoverned by England; were he to exercise "Home Rule," he could rid himself of "dragons" and "root out" sin. A turn inward might have helped him to exercise some small control over his inner life, since his outer life, surrendered in obedience to the Society of Jesus, availed him no surcease. And yet, this possibility was taken away: most scholars believe that someone else wrote those final lines, perhaps after Gerard's death.[18] Or perhaps a friend read the sonnet and offered his continuation as a prescription addressing Gerard's spiritual malady. Not only do those final lines not sound like Gerard, they sound moralizing, and the idea of turning within was in contradiction to how he had always turned to the world "without" to find Christ, but also those verses are not in his handwriting. Consequently, the possibility of hope apparently proffered evaporates, and the poem ends with an admission of failure and a hope for death or, at least, oblivion ("dear forgetfulness").[19] Gerard's condition was quite serious, and worsening. If only he could have found value in his "world within" as he had, so frequently and deeply, found Christ in the world around him. But he could not, would not, love himself: "this is a mournful life to lead," he later wrote, on the first day of the new year, adding the next day, "[I have] nothing to enter but loathing of my life."[20]

Gerard tried to distract himself from his depression by dabbling again in music theory and composition, and he did a bit of sketching. He composed over twenty-seven musical settings for poems, and he attended a few concerts at Trinity, hearing Dvořák's *Stabat Mater* on December 10, 1884, and sight-read and analyzed Purcell's compositions.[21] He was sometimes able to walk about "fine" Phoenix Park, though he found it "inconveniently far off." Gerard also continued to keep up with contemporary English literature, reviling the "overdone reputation" of George Eliot, the author of *Middlemarch*,[22] excoriating Swinburne's most recent publication as "without truth, feeling, or any adequate matter ... some heavydom ... blethery bathos,"[23] and he viewed a private collection of some of Dante Gabriel Rossetti's masterworks.

He continued his correspondence, though he was about to have to share Bridges's attention; Bridges was engaged to be married in August 1884. Gerard made few close friends, but one, a student named Robert Curtis who was studying to become a Jesuit, provided some companionship. A fellow in the natural sciences, Curtis was an epileptic, so he had not been allowed to take his final vows.[24] Like Gerard, he was an outsider. Gerard trusted and admired Father Delaney, president of the college, and relied on him for advice and guidance, as well as often turning to Father Colohan of the Society of Jesus. Gerard also became neighborly with several Irish families and established a strong friendship with the McCabe family in Belleville. He went fishing; he plowed a field one day when, on the spur of the moment, seeing a man with his team of oxen, Gerard jumped the fence and offered to help; he sipped some champagne when urged to by well-meaning hosts who fretted over his pale and thin physique; he drew comical caricatures for local children; and he enjoyed learning and repeating Irish dialect and slang.

On December 9, he wrote a playful letter to his sister Kate—as was the case with his letters to mother and father, he adopted a distinct persona and voice for different addressees—in which he humorously imitated the Dubliner accent, but he claimed to despair of having anything of interest or substance to recount: "Im intoirely ashamed o meself. Sure its a wonder I could lave your iligant corspondance so long onanswered. . . . It bates me where to commince, the way Id say anything yed be interistud to hear of."[25] His humor, always edgy, began to become exceedingly sharp, and he veered between hyperactive, almost manic, states and bouts of extreme despondency in which, as he himself diagnosed, "I think that my fits of sadness resemble madness."[26]

Some surcease and temporary stability ensued when, from time to time, kind elderly Miss Cassidy invited Gerard to the old halls of Monasterevan, founded in the fifth century along the River Barrow, where he could stroll in Moore Abbey Wood and pick bluebells and watch birds. Located in County Kildare, an hour's train ride from Dublin, Monasterevan allowed Gerard to make a reposeful retreat; he was grateful for this and referred to his benefactress as "one of the props and struts of my existence," as though he were a building about to tumble down and in need of bolstering.[27] And, in fact, in Dublin, he was. Most of the time, he held himself apart from his colleagues, retired early to his rooms to avoid interaction with other faculty members, rarely left the college grounds, and only infrequently communicated with his family. On the whole, the only relief from drudgery was the occasional visit to the Jesuit establishments of Milltown Park in Dublin or to Clongowes Wood College,[28] or the rare holiday he was allowed to take, one to England in 1885, another to Scotland, to Wales in 1886 in the company of Robert Curtis. But these were brief. And there was always Dublin, and Gerard's own self-detestation, dwelling there, to face upon return.

For five years he toiled at the imposed drudgery. His *Dublin Notebooks* attest to his meticulous record keeping, careful preparation for classes, and the hours he spent burning the midnight candle:[29] "to bed, to bed: my eyes are almost bleeding," he moaned to Bridges.[30] And he actually was a much-appreciated teacher, perhaps because of his unorthodox teaching methods. Colleagues tittered over how, instead of skipping over the rape scenes in classical literature, Gerard would have his students read the scene aloud, and then he, along with them, would emote: "O those poor girls!" he would cry. And he was legendary for his class in which, dramatizing Hector's death, Gerard would throw himself to the floor and encourage students to drag him about the classroom as though he were a corpse being manhandled along the battlement walls of Troy.[31]

Not all was grim. The comic operas of Gilbert and Sullivan distracted Gerard from his depression. He read a good deal of Thomas Hardy, admiring especially the exquisitely choreographed swordplay episode in *Far from the Madding Crowd*, and the scene of conflagration. Gerard also made some literary acquaintances at this time. Through a fairly casual friendship he struck up with Father Matthew Russell, Gerard had the pleasure of being introduced sometime in 1886 to the poet Katherine Tynan, the Irish Nationalist author, whose devotional poetry he much admired. Tynan, born to a dairy-farming family outside of Dublin, had been educated at a Dominican convent and had considered becoming a nun. She began to publish her primarily Irish folklore-inspired poetry in 1878, quickly experiencing success, and made the acquaintance of W. B. Yeats; Yeats advised her to specialize in poetry dealing with Irish Catholicism. She became known especially for the haunting poem "The Wind That Shakes the Barley." Tynan later married an Englishman and moved to London, where the bishop of London, her great admirer, quoted many of her poems in his sermons. Hopkins and Tynan, though they did not know each other well, corresponded. In the four letters extant between the two, it is clear that they were in many ways kindred spirits. He referred to her affectionately as "the blooming Miss Tynan."[32] Gerard also met Yeats, several times, in the studio of the painter J. B. Yeats, the poet's father, but he never much cared for him; Gerard declared himself to be rather put off by the literary lion's ego and unorthodox views.[33]

Scrupulously conscientious to his vows of obedience, Gerard would not even stay for tea unless he had the Society's permission.[34] Nonetheless, he was able occasionally to dine at the home of the McCabes, and he infrequently saw his friends the Paravicinis when they traveled from Oxford to Ireland. The Baron Paravicini had been at Balliol, and his wife, Frances, was the sister of one of Hopkins's former teachers, Robert Williams. The Paravicinis were becoming greatly worried over Gerard's recurring bouts of deep depression and almost self-destructive behavior. They contacted the Society of Jesus later that year in the vain hope of persuading them to recall Gerard to England.[35]

All the while, despite his protestations to the contrary, and although he never said so, other than an oblique reference to a sonnet "written in blood" to Bridges, Gerard was writing. He was writing perhaps the most extraordinary poetry of his career, six poems that—found only after his death and then only in draft form, scribbled on scrap sheets of lined sermon paper—were dubbed the "sonnets of desolation" or the "terrible sonnets" by subsequent readers,[36] so truly terrifying, so horrifyingly self-hating were they. In all of them Gerard scraped and picked at himself like a compulsive self-mutilator; he figured himself as a "potsherd," like the one Job used to scratch the boils afflicting him when God set Satan loose to torture and test him. Gerard had become his own affliction. As he had admitted to Bridges, "madness seem[s] to be making approaches."[37] Gerard labeled this "my disease" and worried that "the melancholy I have all my life been subject to has become of late . . . more distributed, constant, and crippling. . . . My state is much like madness."[38]

Gerard was fighting a form of insanity, and it had an ancient, theological name: abandonment by God.[39] Always before, Christ had been a constant presence, his beloved and admired heroic exemplar, his love and consolation. He had felt and found Christ in nature, in creatures, in beauty, in patterns, whether they be visual, musical, artistic, or organic. Now Christ, "he my peace," was split off from Gerard; he marked this in the verse line with a slash separating "my peace" from Christ "my parting, sword and strife."[40] The phrase recalled the Gospel of Matthew 10:34, where Jesus said, "I come not to bring peace but a sword." But here the dividedness, the wound, is experienced as being directed within—the sword no longer wielded to carve off the believer from the world, but its blade instead stabbing to shatter Gerard's own internal integrity.

The face of God seemed to have withdrawn from him. When it did rarely appear, it was in nightmares, dark, raving dreams of testing and trial and torture and denial. Gerard began to believe that God wanted him to fail, that God himself was denying him inspiration: "All impulse fails me: I can give myself no sufficient reason for going on. Nothing comes: I am a eunuch—but it is for the kingdom of heaven's sake."[41] He wrote, in one of the terrible sonnets entitled "To Seem the Stranger," penned most likely in 1886, that any attempt he made at poetry "heaven's baffling ban / Bars or hell's spell thwarts"; heaven and hell were now in league together against him, he felt. Before he had thought not to publish, to dedicate himself most fully to God ("This to hoard unheard"); in Dublin he began to wish to produce, but what he did write was misunderstood and rejected ("Heard unheeded"): "This to hoard unheard, / Heard unheeded, leaves me a lonely began." The "lonely began" was unavailing, unfruitful, impotent, exhausted. He was tired of striving, tired of trying, tired of life, and his increasingly divided, self-alienated state poignantly expressed itself with fractures even in the words he wrote: "I wéar- / Y of idle a being."[42] And since he could not, would not, hate God, he began to hate himself.

Increasingly, Gerard felt doubled, divided, ontologically incoherent. His vocation and his vows, his poetic calling—nothing held meaning for him. He described this psychological and spiritual state of agony in the poem "My Own Heart," showing how he felt trapped and tortured within himself, by himself; he desperately longed "not [to] live this tormented mind / With this tormented mind tormenting yet."[43] The "tormented" mind is also the tormentor; it is "tormenting" ceaselessly in a vicious cycle of self-reproach. Gerard had written a work entitled "Meditation on Hell" in which he stated, "Let all consider this: we are our own tormentors, for every sin we then shall have remorse and with remorse torment and the torment fire. . . . God punishing [the sinner] through his own guilty thoughts made him seem to suffer in the part that had offended."[44]

The nobility of soul that Gerard had once felt able to attain through prayer, through self-dedication, through the sacraments, was now degraded to a besmirched and spotted self "soul, self; . . . poor Jackself."[45] This Jack was a new character come to populate Gerard's poetic universe, and he was risible, repulsive, a raw wretch. The name Jack meant "man" in Middle English; it signified "Everyman" in medieval literature. Gerard was dealing in different meanings, as he always enjoyed toying with words, enumerating their manifold meanings and diverse derivations in notebooks, then consulting these lists as he wrote his poetry, but this time he was in deadly earnest. Jack was also a common name in fairy tales. Jack was universal: "every man jack." Jack was quintessentially male. Jack was a worker, like a lumberjack or steeplejack, and sometimes a jack was a sailor. These were manual trades, in which Gerard had long been interested, but they were also occupations fairly low on the social scale. A jack in carpentry was a small shim, shorter than any other boards used in the building, evoking Gerard's own diminutive stature. Jack was a knave in a suit of cards, a lowly fellow; he could be a token or a game piece to be tossed away. Jack could also signify masturbation and sexual deviance—perhaps the guilty "part that had offended" in Gerard. Jack was worthless; "to know jack about something" signified a dearth of knowledge. Jack was Gerard's alter ego: small man in all his shuddering, shameful sinfulness. Jack would return in the poem "That Nature Is a Heraclitean Fire" as "Jack, joke, poor potsherd."[46]

Gerard's self-disgust began to override all other emotion, tainting each day with darkness. Sometime in 1886, he scrawled a draft of the confessional poem "I Wake and Feel" on another bit of sermon paper. The poem is a dialogue between Gerard and his heart. He describes waking from a dream-tossed night, only to find himself in continued spiritual darkness, even in daylight. All the consolation he had formerly derived from Christ seemed to have slipped away. In his retreat notes a few years later, Gerard was still feeling the same desolation and despair. He wrote of the hope of heaven, of the light that would come to him then, but he was not able to take comfort in the present: "how then can it be pretended there is for those who feel this anything worth calling happiness in this world? There is a happiness, hope, the anticipation of happiness hereafter . . . , but it is not happiness now. It is as if one were dazzled by a spark or star in the dark, seeing it but not seeing by it: we want a light shed on our way and a happiness spread over our life."[47]

In "I Wake and Feel," probably the sonnet "written in blood," Gerard's efforts to reach Christ were unavailing. His poetry amounts to ceaseless laments that go unheard, letters that remain unanswered: "And my lament / Is cries countless, cries like dead letters sent / To dearest him that lives alas! away." The letter kills, says Scripture, and the Spirit gives life. Was Gerard feeling that inspiration had deserted him in what he now viewed as his "dead letters"? He who had beheld Christ so close to him in nature, through the wonders of the world, could not find him in the dark city of Dublin; Christ was no longer immanent for Gerard; though still "dearest," Christ lived far "away." Gerard felt psychically imploded; he was ever conscious of his sin, his gross fleshly nature, and his references to his physicality, seemingly unredeemed, became obsessively frequent, expressing his repulsion for his own self: "I am gall, I am heartburn. God's most deep decree / Bitter would have me taste; my taste was me."[48] That taste of self was sin, an unwanted absorption in self that obstructed focus on God and undermined his faith, a spiritual involution that could not escape the material body, its excretions and its failures.[49] Gerard wrote later, identifying self with sin, "The body cannot rest when it is in pain nor the mind be at peace as long as something bitter distills in it and it aches. This may be at any time and is at many."[50] "Something bitter," "heartburn" and "gall," the acid ferment of man without God: "Selfyeast of spirit a dull dough sours."[51]

Believing himself abandoned by God, Gerard had entered into his own personal hell, himself the curse: "The lost are like this, and their scourge to be / As I am mine, their sweating selves; but worse."[52] The semicolon announces that "worse" might yet come in this spiritual struggle, and in the sonnet entitled "No Worst," Gerard showed that was the case. He wrote in a series of negations: "No worst, there is none." Looking into the void, staring into the abyss of life without God, he found utter emptiness, a lack of meaning, no consoling relationship: he cried, "Comforter, where, where is your comforting?"[53] He found no way to confer significance on the actions and gestures of his daily existence. His intellect, formerly his tool for fashioning a theology of beauty, was his ultimate torturer and the agent of his "fall": "O the mind, mind has mountains; cliffs of fall / Frightful, sheer, no-man-fathomed. Hold them cheap / May who ne'er hung there."[54] Gerard hung there, in the space of his own mind, as though crucified. He spewed out his utter scorn for himself at the end of the poem, incorporating the punishment he thought he deserved, spitting it back out at himself: "Here! creep, / Wretch."[55]

On February 17, 1887, he wrote to Bridges, "Tomorrow morning I shall have been three years in Ireland, three hard wearying wasting wasted years,"[56] the repeated *w*'s of the alliterative sentence making flaccid washing sounds, like his life was dribbling away. Worse, he admitted, "But out of Ireland I should be no better, rather worse probably," because at least in Ireland he had been set to some regimen. He began actively to fantasize about dying. Interestingly, given the earlier positive reception of his two shipwreck poems, the death he imagined came in a shipwreck: "The ship I am sailing in may perhaps go down in the approaching gale: if so I shall probably be cast up on the English coast."[57]

No tall nun, no strong sailor, he; Gerard would simply be cast up, like flotsam. Cast up. Abandoned by God.

That same year, Gerard wrote the final version of another of the sonnets of desolation, "(Carrion Comfort)," which he had begun on August 23, 1885, about the same time he had drafted "Times Are Nightfall." The distress, despair, and undoing of that sonnet continue in "(Carrion Comfort)," but here they are intensified: Despair appears as a personification, a prevailing force and presence contending with him. Gerard addresses Despair directly, denies and refuses it, but it overmasters him: "Not, I'll not, carrion comfort, Despair, not feast on thee; / Not untwist—slack they may be—these last strands of man / In me ór, most weary, cry *I can no more*. I can; / Can something, hope, wish day come, not choose not to be."[58] In his desperation to deny Despair, Gerard grasps at possibilities that turn out merely to be negations; his best strategy, to "not choose not to be," is a double negation that simply underscores the temptation to suicide. He had preached in the past, and reminded himself during his retreats, when in his most "desolate"[59] moods, that "hope is an anchor cast in heaven: as long as you do not let it go, hold it must and lost you cannot be."[60] But Gerard had now let hope slip through his fingers. The landscape of "(Carrion Comfort)" is utterly blasted, laid waste. And his inner landscape, too, has been devastated: "But ah, but O thou terrible, why wouldst thou rude on me / Thy wring-earth right foot rock? lay a lionlimb against me? / . . . me heaped there; me frantic to avoid thee and flee?"[61] The verse's "override"[62] scans on to the next line, pinning pathetic Gerard helplessly beneath the right foot that straddles over from the previous line ("why wouldst thou rude on me / Thy wring-earth right foot rock?"). Gerard is helpless ("me heaped there"). At the end of the poem he recounts having once wrestled, like Jacob with the angel, but unlike him, obtained no blessing: "That night, that year / Of now done darkness I wretch lay wrestling with (my God!) my God."[63] The unusual typographic decision to put both the title "(Carrion Comfort)" and the interjection "(my God!)" in parentheses creates a relationship between the two and, horrifyingly, identifies *God* as the carrion comfort. For Gerard, in this sonnet, God himself was the ultimate dealer of despair and death. God had refused him his presence; God had denied productivity and joy to Gerard; God actively sought to bring about his death.

Two months before Gerard died, Frances Paravicini wrote to Robert Bridges, "My husband was in Dublin for a few days before Easter, & he saw Father Gerard once or twice. He thought him looking very ill & said that he was much depressed."[64] Only a month before his death, Gerard was still pleading with God: "birds build—but not I build; no, but strain, / Time's eunuch, and not breed one work that wakes. / Mine, O thou lord of life, send my roots rain."[65] Gerard was struggling mightily. The letters he wrote to Bridges during these last few months were so strange, so insulting, so filled with ranting and self-loathing, that Bridges would not keep them. He burned them.

Yet, a sort of epiphany, a realization that would carry Gerard through and beyond death, that would enable him to cry out, as he was dying, "I am so happy! I am so happy!," had come to him only a few months before he died, and, although the wild oscillation of his moods could not maintain this comfort steadily, it flickeringly sustained him until his final day. The poem "That Nature Is a Heraclitean Fire and of the Comfort of the Resurrection," one of the most extraordinary of all of Gerard's sonnets and most emphatically—and unusually, for his present circumstances—*not* a sonnet of desolation, amounted to a breakthrough for Gerard, both theologically and personally. He wrote it shortly after a much-longed-for vacation to Hampstead, England, his childhood home.[66]

In the stretches of meadows, in the lambent British summer sunshine, Gerard somehow reconnected with what he had found in nature as a boy, and as a young Jesuit enamored of the theology of Scotus. He even expressed his insight propositionally ("That Nature Is . . ."), as Scotus had formulated his propositions about the nature of God, man, and creatures. The reference to Heraclitus harkens back to Gerard's time as a student at Oxford, studying the classics, and especially loving Greek philosophy, under the tutelage of Pater. Heraclitus was a fifth-century BCE pre-Socratic vitalist who believed that the universe was in constant flux. His metaphor for this energetic process of becoming was fire, and he referred to the concept of "soul" as a spark of fire. He had, too, a deep belief in the unity of opposites. Gerard remembered Heraclitus as he wrote, "Million-fuelèd, | nature's bonfire burns on. / But quench her bonniest, dearest | to her, her clearest-selvèd spark / Man, how fast his firedint, | his mark on mind, is gone!"[67]

Gerard transcribed his experience upon his return to Dublin. He noted that his muse unexpectedly had returned to him, having been absent some time while, as he put it in a homely and quasi-comical image, she had spurned him and occupied herself as a laundress: "It is raining now; when is it not? However there was one windy bright day between floods last week: fearing for my eyes, with my other rain of papers, I put work aside and went out for the day, and conceived a sonnet. Otherwise my muse has long put down her carriage and now for years 'takes in washing,'"[68] Gerard wrote to Dixon. His tone was altered; although he was still overworked, exhausted, he sounded almost lighthearted, and he spoke of his muse with almost relaxed affection. Something had happened; something in him had changed.

His spiritual and poetic breakthrough, perhaps propelled by psychic desperation, effected by this trip back to England, among his family and his memories and his beloved countryside, was effectively a return to the beginning, to what he had always known and believed but, in his dark despair, had allowed himself to forget, had ceased to hope for or even to believe in. It allowed him to love his "poor Jackself" to which, until then, he had been denying the hope of redemption. Gerard seems to have now understood Jack suddenly in a universal sense as all men, everyman: Gerard realized that Christ was the ultimate Everyman, who hung on the cross for the sins of all men, who redeemed the world. The cosmic Christ Gerard had sought and loved in nature was now his great friend returned to him in fellowship. Jesus had taken on Jack in this joyous transformation, conceived, in true Scotist fashion, as an act of love rather than necessity; in the "happy exchange"[69] effected between God and man, Jack *was* Jesus.

Gerard put on Christ, clothed his jack self in Jesus's saving act, and, clay and dust compressed through the blinding flash and fire of the resurrection, became—though at first he could hardly dare to believe it—"immortal diamond." "Flesh fade, and mortal trash / Fall to the residuary worm; | world's wildfire, leave but ash: / In a flash, at a trumpet crash, / I am all at once what Christ is, | since he was what I am, and / This Jack, joke, poor potsherd, | patch, matchwood, immortal diamond, / Is immortal diamond."[70]

The realization crashed in on Gerard as he listed Jack's despicable attributes; matchwood was scrap, kindling, broken bits of wood good for nothing else. And yet, matchwood could start a fire, was needed to ignite a blaze. Suddenly, Gerard shifted from the image of matchwood to immortal diamond—a leap of logic, a union of opposites through the redemptive exchange of essences, the joyful jumping up of the resurrected Christ. Gerard seemed only to realize fully the import of what he was writing as he wrote it. The repetition of "immortal diamond" sounds, at first, almost incredulous: "patch, matchwood, immortal diamond, / Is immortal diamond." Then it becomes definitive, salvific. As coal calcined down under heat and pressure and became diamond, so too could Gerard Jack be transformed into the image of Jesus Christ. The agony of separate selfhood, an unacceptable *haeccitas*, was resolved in the acceptance and embrace of Christ for all, absolute being: "*Is* immortal diamond."

I say more: the just man justices;
 Keeps grace: that keeps all his goings graces;
Acts in God's eye *what in God's eye he is*—
 Christ. For Christ plays in ten thousand places,
Lovely in limbs, and lovely in eyes not his
 To the Father through the features of men's
  faces.[71]

Omega: Immortal Diamond

HE HAD TAKEN a trip to his beloved Wales in January 1889, then returned to make a retreat at Tullabeg in County Offaly, Ireland. His last correspondence and his final poem, sent April 29, were both written to the friend of his heart, Bridges. To him only, Gerard confessed ruefully what he believed to be his continued barrenness of inspiration, excusing it as blighted by "my winter world, that scarcely breathes that bliss."[1]

On May 4 Gerard complained of a fleabite, which later turned into a rough red rash covering his body—typhoid, not fleas. He died of peritonitis secondary to typhoid fever, probably from salmonella bacteria contracted through the inadequate treatment of sewage in Dublin and around the university. In an already frail state, he nonetheless lingered six weeks after the disease was diagnosed. Gerard Manley Hopkins departed this life on June 8, 1889, shortly after receiving extreme unction and last rites. The brief obituary read, "He had a most subtle mind, which too quickly wore out the fragile strength of his body."[2]

It ended as it had begun. The small boy, master of mysteries, decoder of the wonders of nature and minstrel to the glory of God, the Gerard as he had been in Hampstead, England, returned at the end. He had been alone often as a child, his father usually away from home; and at the end Gerard was mostly alone,

attended only by a Jesuit father. But Gerard's own father came for
the small ceremony at St. Francis Xavier Church and stood by
the grave as his son was laid to rest in Glasnevin Cemetery, Dublin.[3] Only his father represented the Hopkins family. The Jesuits
burned many of Gerard's papers the morning after his death.[4] He
was gone from the world.

"This world then is word, expression, news of God. Therefore
its end, its purpose, its purport, its meaning, is God and its life or
work to name and praise him. . . . The world, [and] man, should
after its own manner give God being in return for the being he
has given it or should give him back that being he has given."[5] So
Gerard had written, once. And so he now did.

Dust to dust. Dust transmuted to diamond.

Acknowledgments

GRATITUDE TO FATHER Brian Mulcahy, OP, rector of St. Denis Roman Catholic Church in Hanover, New Hampshire, who inadvertently gave me the title for this book.

Thanks to all my Dartmouth students over the past seven years, who swelled my classes on spirituality, mysticism, and religion and literature, and who always heard at least one of Hopkins's poems during each term. Their enthusiasm and insights were invaluable.

Thanks to Rob and Teresa Oden, Peggy and Bob Baum, Katharine Britton, Laura Cousineau, and so many other colleagues and/or dear friends, for offering encouragement.

Thanks to Dartmouth for funding some of the research for this book.

Notes

1. The poem is an affirmation of the doctrine of transubstantiation, a matter of belief crucial in Gerard's conversion to the Roman Catholic faith. See Joseph Feeney, SJ, *The Playfulness of Gerard Manley Hopkins* (London: Ashgate, 2008), for more on the tenor and intent of Gerard's translation, done his first year at St. Beuno's, Wales, and called by him "S. Thomae Aquinatis Rhythmus ad SS. Sacrementum." The poem can be found in *The Major Works, Including All the Poems and Selected Prose*, ed. Catherine Phillips (London: Oxford University Press, 2002), 104–5.

PREFACE

1. "The impatience of this breaking through to the uniquely true glory determines Hopkins' whole ethos; here lies the unity of the personality as poet and religious, that unity of which he was most sharply conscious even when it finally broke him, for neither his poet friends nor his brothers in religion had any eyes for it." Hans Urs von Balthasar, *The Glory of the Lord: A Theological Aesthetics,* vol. 3, *Studies in Theological Style: Lay Styles* (San Francisco: Ignatius, 1986), 357.

2. Why another biography of Gerard Manley Hopkins at this time, when there have been many, some of recent date, and all competent and thorough? Each has taken a particular perspective, explored a specific angle of inquiry of interest to Gerard's readers. Paul Mariani's, the most recent biography (Viking, 2008), beautifully written along the lines

of the acclaimed writer Ron Hansen, offers an experimentally poetic exploration rather than a scholarly work. Julia Saville's sensitive *Queer Chevalier* and Robert Bernard Martin's very readable and thorough 1991 *Gerard Manley Hopkins: A Very Private Life*, to a lesser extent, place a homoerotic emphasis on Gerard's life. Others have been fascinated with Gerard's mood swings and have hypothesized that Gerard was bipolar, if not unipolar, or manifestly depressive, all his life. Norman White's 1992 *A Literary Biography*, adroitly literary-critical, leaves to one side the theological emphases in Hopkins's work. Alan Heuser's 1958 *The Shaping Vision of Gerard Manley Hopkins* offers a unique, spiritual slant on how Gerard composed; however, it is a stylistic study, not a sustained biography. Father Devlin, SJ, characterizes psychologically Gerard's fraught, ambivalent yet also religiously obedient, self-surveillance over poetic production. Gerard, heeding the concerns about secular authorship of the Society of Jesus, which, with one exception, discouraged publication of his poetry, at least for seven years ceased writing poetry. It would take time and experience for him to begin to discern how and why his poetic production could appropriately magnify the Lord.

3. Balthasar, *Glory of the Lord*, 3:357, 393.

4. See Walter Ong's brilliant study of the notion of "selving" in Hopkins. Each self is a distinct entity and seeks dialogue with and fulfillment in other selves—above all, for Hopkins, in the Supreme Self, or Christ. Ong, *Hopkins, the Self, and God* (Toronto: University of Toronto Press, 1980).

5. Hopkins, "Notes on Suarez," in *The Major Works, Including All the Poems and Selected Prose*, ed. Catherine Phillips (London: Oxford University Press, 2002), 285; emphasis original (hereafter *MW*). For purposes of convenience and availability, I have chosen to quote primarily from the 2002 Phillips edition (*MW*) because it is more accessible to the nonspecialist reader and more appropriate to the generalist reader's purposes: it is one volume, paperback, as well as comprehensive and helpfully annotated. For the specialist reader, I highly recommend the authoritative and scholarly *Collected Works of Gerard Manley Hopkins*, ed. Leslie Higgins, Michael Suarez, SJ, Catherine Phillips, et al., vols. 1–8 (Oxford: Oxford University Press, 2006–2018). Occasionally, I quote from other, earlier editions (such as Sir Humphrey House, ed., *The Journals and Papers of Gerard Manley Hopkins* [Oxford: Oxford

University Press, 1959]), and they are so noted. See also *The Sermons and Devotional Writings of Gerard Manley Hopkins*, ed. Christopher Devlin, SJ (Oxford: Oxford University Press, 1967), 134.

6. Hopkins, journal entry, May 11, 1868, in *MW*, 193.

7. One very important effect of Gerard's reading of Scotus was his embracing of a positive theology of the redemption, in which the crucifixion could not be construed as a sacrifice meant to appease a vengeful God; rather, the crucifixion had been part of divine providence from all eternity and was a supreme act of love. See Jack Mahoney, SJ, *Christianity in Evolution* (Washington, DC: Georgetown University Press, 2011).

8. Hopkins, "Pied Beauty," ll. 6–9, 1, 2, in *MW*, 132–33.

9. Consult the brilliant study by Philip A. Ballinger, *The Poem as Sacrament: The Theological Aesthetic of Gerard Manley Hopkins*, Louvain Theological and Pastoral Monographs 26 (Louvain: Peeters; Grand Rapids: Eerdmans, 2000).

10. See, for instance, the Roman Catholic catechism written under Pope Pius X, article 315, in which it is stated that "there are two differences between the Sacraments and sacramentals: (1) the Sacraments were instituted by Jesus Christ, while sacramentals have come to be endorsed by the Church; (2) the Sacraments give Grace in and of themselves . . . whereas sacramentals cause pious dispositions to be born in us through which we may obtain Grace" (author's translation). Other examples of sacramentals are holy water, the sign of the cross, the Angelus prayer, and the rosary.

11. Hopkins to Bridges, January 4, 1883, in *MW*, 257. "Dividing a compound word by a clause sandwiched into it was a desperate deed, I feel." *MW*, 383.

12. Hopkins to Bridges, May 30, 1878, in *Selected Poems*, ed. Bob Blaisdell (Mineola, NY: Dover, 2011), 56. Also: "No doubt my poetry errs on the side of oddness," Hopkins to Bridges, February 15, 1879, in *MW*, 235; "You see then what is against me, but since . . . there is a time for everything . . . it may be that the time will come for my verses," Hopkins to Dixon, December 1, 1881, in *MW*, 251.

13. *The Journals and Papers of Gerard Manley Hopkins*, 134. Also: ". . . like a new witness to God," Hopkins, journal entry, September 24, 1870, 203; further discussed in Martin DuBois, *Gerard Manley Hopkins*

and the Poetry of Religious Experience (Cambridge: Cambridge University Press, 2017), 129.

14. Ballinger, *The Poem as Sacrament*, 149, has argued that Gerard found in Scotus "the possibility of making poetry a theology."

15. There is evidence that Gerard was drawn to Eastern patristic mystics, such as Maximus the Confessor, Saint Macarius, and Saint Gregory Palamas. See Trent Pomplun, "The Theology of Gerard Manley Hopkins: From John Duns Scotus to the Baroque," *Journal of Religion* 95, no. 1 (January 2015): 1–34. Gerard's Jesuit classmates jokingly nicknamed Gerard "Simeon Stylites" due to his predilection for the writings of the desert fathers and the early Christian church. The "Cosmic Christ" is a term prevalent in Eastern Orthodoxy for the God who redeemed in and through fallen matter, thereby giving value and worth to that matter, even in its fallenness. Gerard is in sympathy with this understanding. See Vladimir Lossky, *The Mystical Theology of the Eastern Church* (Crestwood, NY: St. Vladmir's Seminary Press, 1956), 110–12.

16. Cited in David Wilkes and A. N. Wilson, "Priceless Trove of Poems by English Writer Gerard Manley Hopkins Is Discovered after the Tortured Genius Saved His Handwritten Gems for the World," *London Daily Mail*, November 1, 2018, https://www.dailymail.co.uk/news/article-6344457/Priceless-trove-poems-English-writer-Gerard-Manley-Hopkins-discovered.html.

17. The present manuscript was completed prior to the finding of this treasure trove.

ALPHA: THINGS SEEN AND UNSEEN

1. Hopkins, "The Times Are Nightfall," l. 9, in *The Major Works, Including All the Poems and Selected Prose*, ed. Catherine Phillips (London: Oxford University Press, 2002), 161 (hereafter *MW*).

2. Hopkins, "The Loss of the *Eurydice*," l. 94, in *MW*, 138.

3. Hopkins, "Il Mystico," ll. 35, 47, 59–60, in *MW*, 8.

4. Richard Watson Dixon, one of Gerard's schoolmasters, described him as having "a very meditative and intellectual face." A letter from Dixon, cited in Angus Easson, *Gerard Manley Hopkins*, Routledge Guides to Literature (London: Routledge, 2011), 7.

CHAPTER 1

1. Hopkins, "Think of an Opening Page," in *The Major Works, Including All the Poems and Selected Prose*, ed. Catherine Phillips (London: Oxford University Press, 2002), 30 (hereafter *MW*).

2. A biographical narrative written in 1940 by Sir Humphrey House offers rich detail on Gerard's upbringing and relationships with various members of his family. See Sir Humphrey House, "The Youth of Gerard Manley Hopkins, 1844–1868," *Hopkins Quarterly* 37, no. 2 (Winter-Fall 2010): 1–185.

3. Dixon was an important member of the Brotherhood, a group of artists and thinkers formed in 1853 who, along the lines of the previous Pre-Raphaelite Brotherhood and its veneration of medieval art and liturgy, sought to subordinate all artistic and poetic creation to God. Dixon, an English divine and poet, winner of the Oxford prize in Sacred Poetry while a student there, later published acclaimed volumes of verse, such as *Feathers of the Willow*. His fame nearly won him the position of poet laureate on Tennyson's death.

4. Liddon was to become Pusey's biographer.

5. Hopkins, journal entries, August–September 1864, in *MW*, 186.

6. Gerard's staunch Christianity was a major difference between his thought and that of Pater, who questioned Christianity.

7. Hopkins, "To Oxford," part 1, ll. 6, 8, part 2, l. 14, in *MW*, 62–63. Written April 23, 1865.

8. This also became the case for his letters to Kate and to Manley Hopkins.

9. Robert Scott also maintained the "Collections Book" for Balliol College. This was a detailed recording of exams, lectures, classes, and tutors, for all students.

10. This journal is scrupulously maintained from Lent 1865 to Lent 1866 and includes "transgressions" such as eating a sweet, or drinking too much water, among others perhaps more serious.

11. Robert Bernard Martin provides more detail on this relationship in *Gerard Manley Hopkins: A Very Private Life* (New York: Putnam, 1991). Martin, a professor at Princeton University, was at the time of

publication of his study the only academic to have had unrestricted access to all of Hopkins's private papers and correspondence. See chap. 4.

12. John Henry Newman, *An Essay in Aid of a Grammar of Assent* (Oxford: Oxford University Press, 1985), 40, 41.

13. For more on this intriguing story, see the prefatory piece to the *Meditations and Devotions of the Late Cardinal Newman* (New York: Longmans, Green, 1903).

14. Later, as a Jesuit novice, Gerard also read Newman's highly influential *A Grammar of Assent* and discussed it with like-minded friends. In it, Newman strongly makes the case for belief supported by, yet also surpassing, reason. In *A Grammar of Assent*, Gerard read, "in this day it is all too often taken for granted that religion is one of those subjects on which truth cannot be discovered, and on which one conclusion is pretty much on a level with another. But if religion is to be devotion, and not a mere matter of sentiment, if it is to be made the ruling principle of our lives, if our actions, one by one, and our daily conduct, are to be consistently directed towards an Invisible Being, we need something higher than a mere balance of arguments to fix and control our minds. Communion with the spiritual world presupposes a real hold and habitual intuition of the objects of Revelation, which is certitude" (157).

15. Hopkins, "Il Mystico," ll. 141–142, in *MW*, 10.

16. Margaret Johnson, *Gerard Manley Hopkins and Tractarian Poetry* (London: Ashgate, 1997), is a very helpful source for the influence of Tractarian piety on Gerard.

17. Newman, *A Grammar of Assent*, 158: "as regards the world invisible and visible, we have a direct and conscious knowledge of our Maker, His attributes, His providence, acts, works, and will from nature, and revelation."

18. Initially called the Brotherhood of St. Mary (1844), this very Anglo-Catholic or High Church society was reanimated and renamed by Pusey. Members took vows, among them to recite the Gloria Patri (the prayer to the Trinity) upon arising and before going to bed. They also adopted fairly rigorous dietary limitations and behavioral regulations as a way to give honor to the Trinity.

19. Hopkins, "Floris in Italy," in *MW*, 186.

20. As for the question of Gerard's homosexuality, Angus Easson

states that Gerard did not act on his basic nature (*Gerard Manley Hopkins*, Routledge Guides to Literature [London: Routledge, 2011], 15).

21. More on this practice of such a penance can be found in Martin, *Gerard Manley Hopkins*, as well as in Jill Muller, *Gerard Manley Hopkins and Victorian Catholicism: A Heart in Hiding* (London: Routledge, 2003).

22. Once he joined the Jesuits, Gerard intensified these practices and began to wear a scapular, an intimate religious object concealed in his clothes, as well as to use a "discipline," or small whip applied to quell sinful thoughts.

23. Hopkins, journal entry, January 23, 1866, in *MW*, 189.

24. Hopkins, "Moonless Darkness," ll. 4–5, in *MW*, 77.

25. Jill Muller argues persuasively in *Gerard Manley Hopkins and Victorian Catholicism*, 38–39, however, that Newman would have been less in favor of such obvious signs of religious enthusiasm. Newman tended to distrust extremes and sentimentality. Gerard may have been early influenced—and certainly was as a Jesuit novice—by the reading of Frederick William Faber, a priest who counseled more overt signs and behaviors to attest to the strong emotion with which one experienced faith. Muller also shows that Gerard was drawn to ultramontanist meditational works, such as those of Father Alphonse Liguori (40).

26. An intriguing, if somewhat narrowly focused, study by Finn Fordham, *I Do, I Undo, I Redo: The Textual Genesis of Modernism in Hopkins, Yeats, Conrad, Forster, Joyce, and Wolff* (New York: Oxford University Press, 2010), in the chapter entitled "Hopkins and Compression," calls Gerard "microscophilic" (85) in his attention to detail, but also because of his penchant for writing in a very small, crabbed hand and using up every bit of a piece of paper, even writing at right angles in the margins. Fordham analyzes this strategy as an attempt to compress the suspect self in tiny writing: "the ideal of a waste-free economy of the virtuous self is reflected and produced in a literally compressed texture of the text," as though Gerard were exercising surveillance on his "self" (92).

27. Easson, *Gerard Manley Hopkins*, 17, observes that Gerard's choice of the Society of Jesus over the Benedictines, to whom he was first drawn, or the Franciscans, shows a similar urge to cede to author-

ity, to find the suspect self bound within strictures. Jesuit Catholicism promised a way of life, a discipline and a relationship with authority.

28. Martin, *Gerard Manley Hopkins*, 42.

29. For more on Anglican Ritualism, see Nigel Yates, *Anglican Ritualism in Victorian Britain, 1830–1910* (Oxford: Oxford University Press, 1999).

30. Gerard's father had written him, like King David bemoaning the loss of his son Absalom, "O Gerard, my darling boy, are you indeed gone from me?" *Further Letters of Gerard Manley Hopkins Including His Correspondence with Coventry Patmore*, ed. Claude Colleer Abbott (Oxford: Oxford University Press, 1956), 97.

31. Hopkins, "The Half-way House," ll. 7–8, 17–18, in *MW*, 76.

32. Hopkins, journal entry, July 17, 1866, in *MW*, 191.

33. Hopkins, journal entry, August 22, 1866, in *MW*, 192.

34. Hopkins, journal entry, March 1871, in *MW*, 204; see also *MW*, 192.

35. Hopkins, diverse journals for 1862–1875, in *MW*. See Easson, *Gerard Manley Hopkins*, 61.

36. Hopkins, journal entry, July 15, 1868, in *MW*, 194.

37. Hopkins, journal entry, April 21, 1871, in *MW*, 206–7.

38. Hopkins, "Fragments of Richard," st. 1, l. 18, in *MW*, 49.

39. Hopkins, "The Wreck of the *Deutschland*," ll. 228–230, in *MW*, 117 (emphasis added).

40. Hopkins, journal entries, April 15, 1871, July 15, 1868, in *MW*, 206, 194.

41. Hopkins, "The Beginning of the End," st. 3, ll. 10–14, in *MW*, 65.

42. Hopkins, journal entry, 1863, in *MW*, 185.

43. Hopkins, "The Alchemist in the City," ll. 1–4, in *MW*, 65.

44. See Jan Marsh, *Christina Rossetti: A Writer's Life* (New York: Viking, 1995), 314–16, 429, 446, 452, 504–5.

45. Martin, *Gerard Manley Hopkins*, 73, quoting Hopkins.

46. Dinah Birch, ed., *The Pre-Raphaelites* (Oxford: Oxford University Press, 2009), xx.

47. Martin, *Gerard Manley Hopkins*, 80, quoting Hopkins.

48. James to Logan Piersall Smith, October 27, 1913, in *Letters of Henry James*, ed. Percy Lubbock, vol. 2 (New York: Scribner's Sons, 1920), 337.

49. Hopkins to Bridges, in *The Collected Works of Gerard Manley Hopkins*, ed. Leslie Higgins, Michael Suarez, SJ, Catherine Phillips, et

al., vols. 1–8 (Oxford: Oxford University Press, 2006–2018), 1:95; in Easson, *Gerard Manley Hopkins*, 14.

50. Hopkins, "Myself Unholy," l. 9, in *MW*, 67.

51. Hopkins, "Thee, God, I Come From," ll. 9–12, in *MW*, 169.

52. Hopkins, "Fragments of Castara Victrix," part 3, ll. 5–6, in *MW*, 73.

53. "Where shall the word be found? Where shall the word / Resound? Not here, there is not enough silence. . . ." T. S. Eliot, "Ash Wednesday," in *Collected Poems, 1909–1962* (New York: Harcourt, Brace, 1963), V, ll. 11–12, p. 92.

54. Matthew Arnold, "Scholar Gypsy," in *Arnold's Poems* (London: Longmans, 1853), l. 1.

55. Hopkins, "The Caged Skylark," l. 2, in *MW*, 133; Eliot, "Ash Wednesday," II, l. 5, p. 87.

56. Hopkins, "The Caged Skylark," ll. 12–14, in *MW*, 133.

57. Hopkins's journal quoted in Martin, *Gerard Manley Hopkins*, 104.

58. See, among numerous others, Julia Saville, *Queer Chevalier: The Homoerotic Asceticism of Gerard Manley Hopkins* (Charlottesville: University of Virginia Press, 2000), and Margaret Johnson, *Gerard Manley Hopkins and Tractarian Poetry* (London: Routledge, 2016).

59. Bridges made this comparison, stating that the length of "The Wreck of the *Deutschland*" was Whitman-esque.

60. Martin, *Gerard Manley Hopkins*, 114, quoting Hopkins.

61. Hopkins, "Moonless Darkness," ll. 4–5, 9, in *MW*, 77.

62. Hopkins, "The Earth and Heaven," ll. 6, 16, in *MW*, 77–78.

63. John Gillroy, *Gerard Manley Hopkins* (Humanities-E Books, 2007), talks about Raynal, his influence on Gerard, and Gerard's strong interest in the Benedictines.

64. Hopkins to Newman, August 28, 1866, quoted in G. F. Lahey, SJ, *Gerard Manley Hopkins* (New York: Haskell House, 1969), 34.

65. See Wilfred Meynell, *Cardinal Newman: With Other Portraits* (London: Burns & Oates, 1907), especially chap. 5 on the circumstances of the founding of the Birmingham Oratory.

66. Ian Kerr, "Hopkins and Newman," in www.gerardmanleyhop kins.org/Lectures, 2007.

67. See the description Paul Mariani gives of this choice, as well as the quote from Newman, in *Gerard Manley Hopkins: A Life* (New York: Viking, 2008), 70.

CHAPTER 2

1. Hopkins, "Hope Holds to Christ," ll. 1–4, in *The Major Works, Including All the Poems and Selected Prose*, ed. Catherine Phillips (London: Oxford University Press, 2002), 127 (hereafter *MW*).

2. Some he did not burn until right before deciding to join the Society of Jesus in 1868.

3. Hopkins to Bridges, April 1889, quoted in Finn Fordham, *I Do, I Undo, I Redo: The Textual Genesis of Modernism in Hopkins, Yeats, Conrad, Forster, Joyce, and Wolff* (New York: Oxford University Press, 2010), 84.

4. Hopkins, canceled variants to "Myself Unholy," in *MW*, 320 (note to p. 67).

5. Hopkins, journal entry, May 5, 1868, in *MW*, 193. Robert Bernard Martin provides more detail on this relationship in *Gerard Manley Hopkins: A Very Private Life* (New York: Putnam, 1991), 172, quoting Hopkins.

6. Martin, *Gerard Manley Hopkins*, 172, quoting Hopkins.

7. The issue was dated February 18, 1868.

8. Hopkins, "The Elopement," ll. 35, 19–22, 31–34, 36, in *MW*, 94–95.

9. Martin, *Gerard Manley Hopkins*, 167, quoting Newman.

10. Martin, *Gerard Manley Hopkins*, 171, quoting Hopkins.

11. Martin, *Gerard Manley Hopkins*, 179, quoting Hopkins.

12. Mallen, "From the Archives: 155 Years of *Letters and Notices*," Jesuits in Britain, February 1, 2018, https://www.jesuit.org.uk/blog/archives-155-years-letters-and-notices.

13. For a detailed discussion of Gerard's work at the Oratory School and his decision to become a Jesuit, see Angus Easson, *Gerard Manley Hopkins*, Routledge Guides to Literature (London: Routledge, 2011), 70–80.

14. Hopkins, journal entry, July 11, 1868, in *MW*, 193.

15. Martin, *Gerard Manley Hopkins*, 182, quoting Hopkins.

16. Hopkins's influence by, and differences from, the Romantic poets has been much discussed. He was an early emulator of both Keats and Tennyson, though he ultimately assessed Tennyson's language as "stilted," and was also much inclined to the Pre-Raphaelite poets and their interest in medievalism. Hopkins did not care for Robert Browning, but he enjoyed the popular poetry of Edward Lear. Though he

deemed Wordsworth a "seer," he eschewed Wordsworth's pantheism. For Hopkins, everything always points to God, not to a plurality of divinity. Easson, *Gerard Manley Hopkins*, 27, 60.

17. This apt and evocative characterization is Colley's: see part 2 of Ann Colley, *Victorians in the Mountains: Sinking the Sublime* (London: Ashgate, 2010), 174, 186.

18. For instance, hiking in Valtournanches: "above, a grove of ash or sycomore [*sic*] or both, sprayed all one way like water-weed beds in a running stream, . . . in midst of a slope of meadow slightly pulled like an unsteady and swelling surface of water, some ashes growing in a beautifully clustered 'bouquet' . . . the inward bend of the left-hand stem being partly real, partly apparent." Hopkins, journal entry, July 26, 1868, in *MW*, 197.

19. Angus Easson discusses how Hopkins liked to juxtapose, to put two meanings together side by side and let them rub together. Easson refers to this technique as "counterpointing." *Gerard Manley Hopkins*, 58.

20. Norman MacKenzie, *A Reader's Guide to Gerard Manley Hopkins* (Philadelphia: St. Joseph's University Press, 2008), 21.

21. Hopkins, journal entry, July 11, 1868, in *MW*, 193.

22. MacKenzie, *Reader's Guide to Gerard Manley Hopkins*, 15.

23. Hopkins, journal entry, July 18, 1868, in *MW*, 195.

24. Hopkins, journal entry, August 30, 1867, in *MW*, 192.

25. Marshall McLuhan (The Kenyon Critics, *Gerard Manley Hopkins: A Critical Symposium*, ed. F. R. Leavis [New York: New Directions, 1940], see chap. 2) called Hopkins an "analogist" rather than a mystic, asserting that the mystic experience is typified by a sort of union with radical Otherness, while he means the term "analogist" to describe Hopkins's way of experiencing God through something else, usually nature, rather than a special, enraptured state such as Saint Teresa of Avila entered into. (For an interesting discussion of McLuhan's argument, see Glenn Hughes, *A More Beautiful Question: The Spiritual in Poetry and Art* [Columbia: University of Missouri Press, 2011], 48–53.) Yet, to me, much of Hopkins's poetry indeed seems ecstatic in language and outcry; its ruptured rhythms and atypical vocabulary seem to evoke a state of otherness, of what Michel de Certeau would call "mystic speech" (*The Mystic Fable*, trans. Michael Smith, vol. 1 [Chicago: University of Chicago Press, 1992]). If McLuhan's intent is to normalize Hopkins within the Catholic

faith, I can accept his strategy, as Hopkins was always doctrinally orthodox and an obedient son of the church; he did not ever seek to distinguish
or singularize himself through any "abnormal" spiritual state.

26. Hopkins, "Rosa Mystica," ll. 1–4, in *MW*, 100.

27. Hopkins, "Blessed Virgin," ll. 115, 34–37, 75–81, in *MW*, 159–160.

28. Evelyn Underhill, *The Essentials of Mysticism* (1920; reprint, New
York: Cosimo Classics, 2007): "In the true mystic, who is so often and
so wrongly called a 'religious individualist,' we see personal religion
raised to its highest power. If we accept his experience as genuine, it in-
volves an intercourse with the spiritual world, an awareness of it, which
transcends the normal experience, and appears to be independent of the
general religious consciousness of the community to which he belongs.
The mystic speaks with God as a person with a Person. . . . He lives by
an immediate knowledge . . . bridging the gap which lies between the
ordinary mind and the suprasensuous world" (25, 42).

29. Underhill, *The Essentials of Mysticism*, 55. "But the mystic is not
merely a self going out on a solitary quest of Reality. He can, must, and
does go only as a member of the whole body, performing as it were the
function of a specialized organ. What he does, he does for all. He is, in
fact, an atoner pure and simple: something stretched out to bridge a gap."

30. Martin DuBois, *Gerard Manley Hopkins and the Poetry of Religious Experience* (Cambridge: Cambridge University Press, 2017), 65.
"This is writing which is at once a form of individual self-expression
and at the same time capable of being repeated and reiterated as a type
of ritual."

31. Hopkins, "Blessed Virgin," ll. 86–89, in *MW*, 160.

32. Hopkins, "Rosa Mystica," ll. 4, 25–28, 34, in *MW*, 100–101.

33. Hopkins, journal entry, July 26, 1868, in *MW*, 195–196.

34. Hopkins, journal entry, July 18, 1868, in *MW*, 194.

35. Hopkins, in *MW*, 320 (note to p. 68).

36. Paul Mariani's description of this period in Hopkins's life is invaluable. See his biography, *Gerard Manley Hopkins: A Life* (New York:
Viking, 2008).

37. For scholarly work on Hopkins's Jesuit training, consult Alfred
Thomas, SJ, *Hopkins the Jesuit: The Years of Training* (Oxford: Oxford
University Press, 1969).

38. Bridges, quoted in Martin, *Gerard Manley Hopkins*, 193.

39. Paul Mariani's evocation of this period in Hopkins's life is beautifully written and provides many helpful daily-life details. See *Gerard Manley Hopkins*.

40. H. W. Crocker III, *The Power and the Glory of the Catholic Church* (New York: Three Rivers Press, 2015), is a useful overview.

41. Martin, *Gerard Manley Hopkins*, 202, quoting Hopkins.

42. Hopkins, "Binsey Poplars," ll. 1–5, 9–11, in *MW*, 142.

43. Hopkins, "Inversnaid," ll. 13–16, in *MW*, 153.

44. Hopkins, "For a Picture of Saint Dorothea," ll. 21, 23, in *MW*, 48.

45. Hopkins, journal entries, September 24, 1870, and 1871, in *MW*, 202, 203; see also 209, 211.

46. Hopkins, "Sermon for Sunday Evening Nov. 23 1879," in *MW*, 277.

47. In the sense that "immanentist" theology sees the spiritual world as suffusing the ordinary realm, and as opposed to a "transcendentist" view, which argues that the metaphysical realm is above and separate from material reality.

48. Hopkins, journal entry, December 23, 1869, in *MW*, 199.

49. Hopkins, journal entry, December 23, 1869, in *MW*, 200, 199.

50. At any rate, such is how Hopkins interpreted a similar episode several years later. Hopkins, journal entry, September 18, 1873, in *MW*, 219: "I had a nightmare that night. I thought something or someone leapt onto me and held me quite fast: this I think woke me. . . . This first start is, I think, a nervous collapse."

51. Hopkins, journal entry, December 23, 1869, in *MW*, 200–201.

52. Hopkins, journal entry, 1869, in *MW*, 198; journal entry, 1871, in *MW*, 204.

53. Hopkins, journal entry, 1871, in *MW*, 204.

54. Changing, or ringing musical changes, entails striking different sequences, switching up rhythm and rounds of bell ringing. Gerard was imitating this technique in his poetry, trying out variations and combinations for their tonality and their evocativeness.

55. A good place to start thinking about this phenomenon is from the emergent field of neurotheology, or the relationship between spiritual matters and brain matter, as discussed in William Braud, "Brains,

Science, Nonordinary and Transcendent Experiences: Can Conventional Concepts and Theories Adequately Address Mystical and Paranormal Experiences?," in *NeuroTheology: The Relationship between Brain and Religion*, ed. A. Sayadmansour (Oxford: Oxford University Press, 2012), 123–66.

56. See the discussion of these and other aspects of mysticism in F. Samuel Brainard, "Defining 'Mystical Experience,'" *Journal of the American Academy of Religion* 64, no. 2 (1996): 329–93.

57. Hopkins, journal entry, 1871, in *MW*, 205.

58. There are biblical echoes. See Luke 12:48 (RSV).

59. See Matthew C. Bagger, "Anti-representationalism and Mystical Empiricism," *Method and Theory in the Study of Religion* 20 (2008): 297–307, in which he documents that mystics report states of heightened cognition and awareness rather than an experience (or a loss) of extraordinary consciousness. Hopkins's hyperawareness and sensitivity to the minutest detail, as well as his attempt to parse or understand the experience in some rational way not excluded by the sensual aspect of the event, seem to fit this assessment.

60. Aquinas's "great chain of being" describing a hierarchical universe was analyzed famously by Etienne Gilson in *The Philosophy of Thomas Aquinas* (New York: Dorset, 1948), 152. Point 6 asserts, for instance, that "to posit creatures of different species means necessarily to posit creatures of unequal degrees of perfection."

61. Hopkins, "S. Thomae Aquinatis Rhythmus ad SS. Sacramentum," l. 25, in *MW*, 105.

62. Martin, *Gerard Manley Hopkins*, 206, quoting Hopkins.

63. Although it does not in all respects entirely concur with my discussion of Scotus and Hopkins, valuable scholarship on Hopkins and Scotus includes, among others, Philip Endean, SJ, "The Two Vocations of Gerard Manley Hopkins," *Thinking Faith*, July 11, 2014, https://www.thinking faith.org/articles/two-vocations-gerard-manley-hopkins; and Bernadette Waterman Ward, *World as Word: Philosophical Inquiry in Gerard Manley Hopkins* (Washington, DC: Catholic University Press, 2002).

64. Hopkins, journal entry, August 20, 1880, in *MW*, 282.

65. Hopkins, journal entry, August 20, 1880, in *MW*, 282.

66. Hopkins, "Hurrahing in Harvest," ll. 5–6, 11–12, in *MW*, 134.

67. Martin also notes this stylistic tendency. See *Gerard Manley Hopkins*, 214.

68. Hopkins, journal entry, April 22, 1871, in *MW*, 207 (emphasis added).

69. Hopkins's understanding of Scotus has actually contributed to a radical modern reshaping of Western theology, in that a contemporary Franciscan preaches this understanding of Scotus's theology and, indeed, has himself published on Hopkins. See Richard Rohr, *Immortal Diamond: The Search for Our True Self* (San Francisco: Jossey-Bass, 2003). See also Rohr, "Daily Meditation from the Center for Action and Contemplation," Week Six: Jesus and the Cross, "A Bigger God": Wednesday, February 6, 2019. He quotes Scotus in an epigraph, "Our predestination to glory is *prior* by nature to any notion of sin" (emphasis added). This meditation is an adapted excerpt taken from Rohr's newest book, *The Universal Christ: How a Forgotten Reality Can Change Everything We See, Hope For, and Believe* (New York: Convergent, 2019), 143–45. I thank Randall Balmer, professor of American religious history at Dartmouth College, for pointing out this particular essay.

70. *Catechism* (p. 1670). Further, sacramentals are defined as "sacred signs which bear a resemblance to the sacraments" (*Catechism*, p. 1667). "Sacramentals prepare us to receive Grace and dispose us to cooperate with it" (p. 1667). "These expressions of piety extend the life of the Church but do not replace it" (p. 1675). "Among the sacramentals blessings occupy an important place. They include ... praise of God for His works and gifts" (p. 1678). From *Catechism of the Catholic Church*, 6th ed. (Vatican City: Liberia Editrice Vaticana, 2007), II, 2, article 1: Sacramentals.

71. Martin, *Gerard Manley Hopkins*, 208, quoting Hopkins.

72. Aakanksha Virkar Yates, *The Philosophical Materialism of Gerard Manley Hopkins*, Nineteenth Century Series (London: Routledge, 2018), finds that there was indeed such an influence: "[Following] both the Cappadocian Fathers, Gregory Nazianzen and Gregory of Nysssa ... it is that mystical reshaping of the soul in the image of Christ and God that Hopkins suggests here" (50).

73. Another Eastern patristic writer who would have disposed Hopkins to regard the natural world as the appropriate theater for the ap-

prehension of the incarnation said, "I do not worship matter. I worship the God of matter, who became matter for my sake and deigned to inhabit matter, who worked out my salvation through matter. I will not cease from honoring that matter which works for my salvation." St. John Damascene, quoted in Rohr, *Universal Christ*, 675.

74. There is some evidence that certain parties received Scotus favorably at Hopkins's seminary. See Edward J. Ondrako, ed., *The Newman-Scotus Reader* (Wausaukee, WI: Academy of the Immaculata, 2015).

75. First quoted explicitly in Hopkins's *Devotional Writings* in 1883, but he was clearly already interacting with the concept.

76. See Scotus, *Ordinatio* III, dist. 19.

77. There are numerous references in his journals. One tale he told while at Stonyhurst was that of an Irish football player who was bested by evil fairies in a marvelous football match, but when he invoked the names of the saints and "Our Lady's name" they let him go. Hopkins relates this tale, initially shared with him by another Jesuit, Brother Byrne, without rational dissection of its plausibility or veracity. Journal entry, April 4, 1870, in *MW*, 202.

78. Martin, *Gerard Manley Hopkins*, 225, quoting Hopkins.

79. Trent Pomplun, "The Theology of Gerard Manley Hopkins: From Duns Scotus to the Baroque," *Journal of Religion* 95 (2015): 5, quoting Hopkins, journal entry, August 3, 1872, in *MW*, 211.

80. Martin, *Gerard Manley Hopkins*, 230, quoting Hopkins.

81. Pomplun, "Theology of Gerard Manley Hopkins," 5.

82. Pomplun, "Theology of Gerard Manley Hopkins," 22.

83. The Quadrilateral was a club first founded by John Wesley to uphold "the four-legged stool" of Anglican theology: Scripture, tradition, experience, and reason.

84. Louise Creighton, *Life and Letters of Mandell Creighton* (London: Longmans, Green, 1904).

85. Hopkins to Bridges, August 21, 1877, in *MW*, 227.

86. Elizabeth Campbell, "Gerard Manley Hopkins," in *Victorian Britain: An Encyclopedia*, ed. Sally Mitchell (London: Routledge, 1988), 374.

87. Martin, *Gerard Manley Hopkins*, 222, quoting Hopkins.

CHAPTER 3

1. Ignatius, "Letter 29, May 24, 1541, to Magdalene Loyola," in *Letters of St. Ignatius of Loyola*, trans. William J. Young, SJ (Chicago: Loyola University Press, 1959), 1:170–71.

2. Hopkins, "Sermon for Monday October 25, 1880," in *The Major Works, Including All the Poems and Selected Prose*, ed. Catherine Phillips (London: Oxford University Press, 2002), 278–79 (hereafter *MW*).

3. For more on St. Beuno's, see Dennis Meadows, *Obedient Men: A Moving and Exceptionally Honest Account of the Author's Ten Years as a Jesuit* (reprint, Whitefish, MT: Literary Licensing, 2010).

4. For more on Hansom, see Penelope Harris, *The Architectural Achievement of Joseph Aloysius Hansom (1803–1882): Designer of the Hansom Cab, Birmingham Town Hall, and Churches of the Catholic Revival* (Lewiston, NY: Edwin Mellen, 2009).

5. See Frederick Packard, *The Life of Robert Owen* (Carlisle, MA: Applewood, 2010).

6. For more on the "chapel" designation, consult John Wolffe, *Religion in Victorian England*, vol. 5, *Culture and Empire* (Manchester: Manchester University Press, 1997).

7. "Hopkins is above all always a 'religious' poet . . . [his] poetic resources are directed still to the indwelling presence of God in nature, a sacramental perception, that through nature we can gain God's grace." Angus Easson, *Gerard Manley Hopkins*, Routledge Guides to Literature (London: Routledge, 2011), 27.

8. Hopkins, "The Wreck of the *Deutschland*," ll. 37–39, in *MW*, 111.

9. Robert Bernard Martin, *Gerard Manley Hopkins: A Very Private Life* (New York: Putnam, 1991), 238, quoting Hopkins.

10. At seminary in Lancashire, Gerard had made notes in his journal about various regional pronunciations and emphases in dialect, paying attention specially to phonetic nuances and shifts as well as locally-specific vocabulary. Several of the priests there had European accents, as well, and Gerard had noted those.

11. Hopkins to Dixon, October 5, 1878, in *MW*, 334–35 (note to p. 110).

12. The phrase is Eve Sedgwick's, from *Between Men: English Lit-*

erature and Male Homosocial Desire (New York: Columbia University Press, 1985).

13. *Times* (UK), December 11 and 13, 1875; in *MW*, 338 (note to p. 114).

14. For more on the politics of the *Kulturkampf*, see Gordon Boyce Thompson, *The Kulturkampf: An Essay* (Toronto: University of Toronto Press, 2018).

15. In 1872, the Society of Jesus was believed to be the vanguard of the Catholic Church's ultramontane politics to dominate the German state. See Michael Gross, "Kulturkampf and Unification: German Liberalism and the War against the Jesuits," *Central European History* 30, no. 4 (1997): 540–66.

16. Martin, *Gerard Manley Hopkins*, 258, quoting Bridges.

17. This is Martin's scholarly assessment in *Gerard Manley Hopkins*, 256.

18. Hopkins, "The Wreck of the *Deutschland*," l. 127, in *MW*, 114; ll. 221, 223, 225–226, 247, in *MW*, 117.

19. Hopkins, "The Wreck of the *Deutschland*," ll. 185–188, in *MW*, 116; l. 146, in *MW*, 114; ll. 9–11, 30, 32, in *MW*, 110.

20. Hopkins, "The Wreck of the *Deutschland*," ll. 273–277, in *MW*, 118.

21. I was not able to consult the following study, as this manuscript was completed before its publication, but all indications are that Dr. Ward has a similar understanding to the one I develop on the complementarity of Ruskin and Scotus. Consult Bernadette Waterman Ward, *Gerard Manley Hopkins and Ruskin's Idea of the Christian Artist in Religion and the Arts* (Leiden: Brill, 2018).

22. John Ruskin, "Inaugural Lecture as Slade Professor of Fine Arts," in *John Ruskin: Selected Writings*, ed. Dinah Birch (Oxford: Oxford University Press, 2009), 198.

23. John Ruskin, "Proserpina," in Birch, *John Ruskin*, 251–52.

24. Hopkins, "Notes on Suarez," in *MW*, 287, 283, 284.

25. Hopkins, "Notes on Suarez," in *MW*, 284.

26. Hopkins, "The Wreck of the *Deutschland*," ll. 59–64, in *MW*, 112.

27. Hopkins, "The Windhover," ll. 7–11, in *MW*, 132.

28. Hopkins, "The Windhover," ll. 13–14, in *MW*, 132.

29. Hopkins, "The Windhover," l. 12, in *MW*, 132.

30. Ruskin, "Of Truth of Space," in Birch, *John Ruskin*, 4.

31. Hopkins, "Pied Beauty," l. 10, in *MW*, 133.

32. Hopkins, "The Windhover," l. 12, in *MW*, 132.

33. Duns Scotus, *Duns Scotus on Divine Love: Texts and Commentaries on Goodness and Freedom*, ed. A. Vos and H. Veldhuis (London: Ashgate, 2003), 128.

34. Scotus, *Duns Scotus*, 136.

35. Scotus, *Duns Scotus*, 136.

36. Scotus gave primacy to the will and valued intellect set in relation to the experience of the senses; knowledge was not abstract but deeply and uniquely knowable in each entity. See Douglas Langston, "Scotus's Doctrine of Intuitive Cognition," *Studies in Early Fourteenth Century Philosophy* 96, no. 1 (July 1993): 3–24.

37. Hopkins, "The Wreck of the *Deutschland*," ll. 228–230, in *MW*, 117.

38. Scotus, *Duns Scotus*, 70–71.

39. Scotus, *Duns Scotus*, 118. See Konstantin Koser, "The Basic Significance of Knowledge for Christian Perfection," *Franciscan Studies* 8, no. 2 (June 1948): 153–72. For Scotus, knowledge and perfection are not incompatible. Neither are they for Hopkins.

40. Scotus, *Duns Scotus*, 292–93.

41. Hopkins, journal entry, October 19, 1874, in *MW*, 221.

42. Hopkins, "Pied Beauty," ll. 1–5, 7, in *MW*, 132–33.

43. Hopkins, "Sermon for Monday Evening Oct. 24 1880," in *MW*, 279.

44. Hopkins, "Hurrahing in Harvest," ll. 5–6, 9, 11–12, 13–14, in *MW*, 134.

45. John 1:5 (KJV and Douay-Rheims).

46. Hopkins, "The Lantern out of Doors," ll. 5–6, 10–11, 12–13, in *MW*, 134.

47. Trent Pomplun, "The Theology of Gerard Manley Hopkins: From John Duns Scotus to the Baroque," *Journal of Religion* 95, no. 1 (January 2015): 33, deems this neo-Thomism "strident."

48. Scotus, *Duns Scotus*, 118.

49. For more on this, see Joseph F. Feeney, SJ, *The Playfulness of Gerard Manley Hopkins* (London: Routledge, 2008). See in particular the chapters on Hopkins's religious formation. Here, and in others of his scholarly works, Feeney discusses why Hopkins did not do a fourth

year of theology and looks at his frequent reassignments to different Jesuit parishes and institutions.

50. Hopkins, "Brothers," ll. 41–43, in *MW*, 152.

51. Robert Darby, in *The Demonization of the Foreskin and the Rise of Circumcision in Britain* (Chicago: University of Chicago Press, 2005), referring to the *Encyclopaedia Britannica*, 9th ed., vols. 1–24 (1888). Darby mentions the "pathologizing" of the penis.

52. A nonretractable foreskin, which can cause irritation and infection. Medical journals often cannot distinguish initially between a physiological and a psychological, or pathological, explanation for the phenomenon. J. S. Huntley et al., "Troubles with the Foreskin," *Journal of Social Medicine* 96, no. 9: 449–51.

53. Hopkins, "The Loss of the *Eurydice*," ll. 105, 98, in *MW*, 138; ll. 77–80, in *MW*, 137; ll. 94, 113–116, in *MW*, 138.

54. Hopkins, "May Magnificat," ll. 45–48, in *MW*, 140; ll. 16–18, 30–32, 13, 17, 27–28, 25, in *MW*, 139; ll. 43–44, in *MW*, 140.

55. Easson, *Gerard Manley Hopkins*, 31.

56. Easson, *Gerard Manley Hopkins*, 28.

57. Francis Baron de Paravicini had been at Balliol. His wife engaged in some correspondence with Hopkins's mother near the end of his life.

58. Eric G. Tenbus, *English Catholics and the Education of the Poor, 1807–1902* (London: Routledge, 2016), 5–6. Tenbus emphasizes that much of this attitude on the part of the Irish Catholic immigrants came from a strong desire to hold themselves apart and to not be assimilated.

59. Hopkins to Bridges, July 1878, in *MW*, xxix.

60. Hopkins, "Binsey Poplars," ll. 1, 21, 12–13, 9–11, 19, 22–24, in *MW*, 142–43.

61. Quoted by Antonia Fraser in *Royal Charles: Charles II and the Restoration* (New York: Knopf, 1979), 33.

62. Hopkins to Bridges, August 14, 1879, in *MW*, 240.

63. Hopkins to Dixon, November 2, 1881, in *MW*, 249.

64. Martin, *Gerard Manley Hopkins*, 310, quoting Hopkins.

65. For more on this, see Norman MacKenzie, ed., *The Poetical Works of Gerard Manley Hopkins, 1844–1889* (Oxford: Clarendon, 1990).

66. Hopkins, journal entry, October 8, 1874, in *MW*, 221.

67. Hopkins to Bridges, Feruary 15, 1879, in *MW*, 235.

68. Martin, *Gerard Manley Hopkins*, 313, quoting Dixon.

69. Sebastian Evans and T. E. Brown, "R. W. Dixon," in *The Cambridge History of English and American Literature in 18 Volumes (1907–21)*, vol. 13, *The Victorian Age* (Cambridge: Cambridge University Press, 2000), #41, 76.

70. Hopkins to Bridges, October 18, 1882, in *MW*, 254.

71. Hopkins to Dixon, October 1879, quoted in *MW*, xxxi.

72. Hopkins to Dixon, December 1, 1881, in *MW*, 250.

73. See Alexander Tulloch, *The Story of Liverpool* (Gloucestershire: History Press, 2008).

74. Hopkins to Bridges, October 26, 1880, quoted in *MW*, xxxi.

75. Hopkins, quoted in *MW*, xxxi.

76. Martin, *Gerard Manley Hopkins*, 325.

77. Hopkins, "Felix Randal," ll. 9–11; l. 8, the phrase "God rest him all road ever he offended" translates as "God forgive him all his sins"; l. 14, in *MW*, 150.

78. Hopkins to Dixon, December 22, 1880, in *MW*, 244.

79. Hopkins, "Spring and Fall," ll. 2, 5–8, 9, 12–13, 14–15, in *MW*, 152.

80. Hopkins to Bridges, September 16, 1881, in *MW*, 245.

81. Michael Doyle, *Communal Violence in the Empire: Disturbing the Pax* (London: Bloomsbury, 2017).

82. Michael Meighan, *Glasgow: A History* (London: Amberley Books, 2013).

83. Hopkins, journal entry, undated, during the winter of 1880–1881, quoted in *MW*, xxxi.

84. Hopkins, "Inversnaid," ll. 4, 8, 1–2, 13–15, in *MW*, 153.

85. Hopkins to Bridges, October 28, 1886, in *MW*, 265.

86. Martin, *Gerard Manley Hopkins*, 338, quoting Hopkins.

87. See Peter Schineller, SJ, "Jesuit Glossary," at www.sjweb.info/arsi/documents/glossary.pdf, where the significance of the fourth vow is explained, along with other terms relevant to the Society of Jesus.

88. Martin, *Gerard Manley Hopkins*, 247, quoting Hopkins.

89. Hopkins to Bridges, January 4, 1883, in *MW*, 257.

90. It should be noted that the poem reasserted Victorian gender norms. Women were seen as paragons of domesticity, and the cantos of the poem chart the course of an idealized marriage. Patmore became

a Roman Catholic shortly after Emily's death in 1862, and his poem became one of the most popular of the Victorian era.

91. Hopkins, quoted in John J. Dunn, "Love and Eroticism," *Victorian Poetry* 7, no. 3 (1969): 203.

92. Martin, *Gerard Manley Hopkins*, 357, quoting Hopkins.

93. Hopkins to Bridges, January 4, 1883, in *MW*, 257.

94. Hopkins to Bridges, March 7, 1884, in *MW*, 259–60.

CHAPTER 4

1. Hopkins, "As Kingfishers Catch Fire," ll. 1–8, in *The Major Works, Including All the Poems and Selected Prose*, ed. Catherine Phillips (London: Oxford University Press, 2002), 129 (hereafter *MW*).

2. Hopkins, retreat notes, January 5, 1889, in *MW*, 304. These notes were written while Hopkins was in Tullabeg.

3. Michael Barry, *Victorian Dublin Revealed: The Remarkable Legacy of Nineteenth-Century Dublin* (Dublin: Andalus, 2018).

4. Hopkins, retreat notes, January 1, 1889, in *MW*, 303.

5. Hopkins to Bridges, August 21, 1884, in *MW*, 261.

6. Hopkins to Bridges, March 7, 1884, in *MW*, 260.

7. Hopkins to Bridges, September 1, 1885, in *MW*, 264.

8. Robert Bernard Martin, *Gerard Manley Hopkins: A Very Private Life* (London: Faber & Faber, 2011), 356, quoting a faculty member.

9. Hopkins to Bridges, September 1, 1885, in *MW*, 263–64.

10. For more on this, see the study of Gladstone by Richard Cook, *Grand Old Man* (Dodo Press, 1898).

11. Grenfall Morton, *Home Rule and the Irish Question* (London: Routledge, 2014).

12. Fiona MacCarthy, *William Morris: Between Anarchy and Beauty, 1860–1960* (London: National Portrait Gallery, 2014); Fiona MacCarthy, *William Morris: A Life for Our Time* (London: A&U, 1994). Morris was, in fact, the founding member of the British Socialist Party.

13. Allison Sulloway, "Gerard Manley Hopkins and 'Women and Men' as 'Partners in the Mystery of Redemption,'" *Gerard Manley Hopkins: A Centenary Celebration* (University of Texas), Spring 1989, 31–51.

14. See H. W. J., "Our Book Table," *Christian Socialist: A Journal for Those Who Work and Think* 9 (August 1891): 89.

15. Hopkins to Bridges, October 13, 1886, in *MW*, 264.

16. Hopkins to Bridges, July 30, 1887, in *MW*, 269; February 17, 1887, in *MW*, 267, 268.

17. Hopkins, "The Times Are Nightfall," ll. 1–2, 5–8, 9–11, in *MW*, 161.

18. The copy is not definitive. Some verses are scrawled on Royal University of Ireland letterhead. Catherine Phillips notes that "Hopkins does not appear to have written the sonnet's final three lines." In *MW*, 371 (note to p. 161).

19. Hopkins, "The Times Are Nightfall," l. 8, in *MW*, 161.

20. Hopkins, retreat notes, January 1 and 2, 1889, in *MW*, 303.

21. "I hope Purcell is not damned for being a Protestant, because I love his genius . . . his own individuality . . . his individual markings and mottlings, 'the sakes of him.'" Hopkins to Bridges, January 5, 1883, in *MW*, 258.

22. Hopkins to Bridges, October 28, 1886, in *MW*, 265.

23. Hopkins to Bridges, April 29, 1889, in *MW*, 272.

24. Michael McGinley, "Hopkins' Friends in Dublin," Hopkins Lectures 2016, at https://www.jesuitica.be/research/view/item/20601/.

25. Hopkins to sister Kate, December 9, 1884, in *MW*, 262.

26. Martin, *Gerard Manley Hopkins*, 381, quoting Hopkins.

27. Hopkins to Bridges, April 29, 1889, in *MW*, 273.

28. Michael Flecky, SJ, *Hopkins in Ireland: Pictures and Words* (Omaha: Creighton University Press, 2008).

29. *The Collected Works of Gerard Manley Hopkins*, ed. Leslie Higgins, Michael Suarez, SJ, Catherine Phillips, et al., vols. 1–8 (Oxford: Oxford University Press, 2006–2008); here see vol. 7, *The Dublin Notebooks* (Oxford: Oxford University Press, 2014).

30. Hopkins to Bridges, January 12, 1888, in *MW*, 271.

31. Some assessments do not concur. Compare the view of Simon Edge in "Gerard Manley Hopkins, a Terrible Teacher," *Irish Times*, May 22, 2017. Edge concludes that Hopkins "loathed his work with a vengeance" and "could not control his students."

32. Hopkins to Bridges, February 17, 1887, in *MW*, 266.

33. Matthew Campbell, *Irish Poetry under the Union: 1801–1924* (Cambridge: Cambridge University Press, 2013). See especially chap. 7,

"Spelt from Sibyl's Leaves: Hopkins, Yeats, and the Unraveling of British Poetry."

34. Another Jesuit, Father Goldie, reported this. *MW*, 396 (note to p. 263).

35. This was on or just after April 21, 1888. See the very helpful discursive description of the recently edited and published correspondence in Paul Mariani's review, "*The Collected Works of Gerard Manley Hopkins* Vols. I and II, ed. R. K. R. Thornton and Catherine Phillips," *Journal of Jesuit Studies* 1, no. 3 (2014): 504–10.

36. Hilary Peterson, "The 'Terrible Sonnets' of Gerard Manley Hopkins," *Way* 46, no. 1 (January 2007): 23–37.

37. Hopkins to Bridges, September 1, 1885, in *MW*, 264.

38. Martin, *Gerard Manley Hopkins*, 395, quoting Hopkins.

39. This is a concept subsumed under the rubric of moral theology, and it has a long-standing tradition. In the earliest days of the Christian church, Eusebius of Caesarea wrote about it. Saint Paul talked about it in the Epistle to the Romans. Saint Thomas Aquinas wrote about it in his *Commentary on the Gospel of John*. See "18th- and 19th-Century Ignatian Voices," Ignatian Spirituality, https://www.ignatianspirituality.com /ignatian-voices/18th-and-19th-century-ignatian-voices/, for more on the Society of Jesus's understanding of what it meant to be abandoned by God.

40. Hopkins, "To Seem the Stranger," l. 4, in *MW*, 166.

41. Hopkins to Bridges, January 12, 1888, in *MW*, 270.

42. Hopkins, "To Seem the Stranger," ll. 12–13, 13–14, 7–8, in *MW*, 166.

43. Hopkins, "My Own Heart," ll. 3–4, in *MW*, 170.

44. Hopkins, "Meditation on Hell," in *MW*, 293.

45. Hopkins, "My Own Heart," l. 9, in *MW*, 170.

46. Hopkins, "That Nature Is a Heraclitean Fire and of the Comfort of the Resurrection," l. 23, in *MW*, 181.

47. Hopkins, retreat notes, January 2, 1889, in *MW*, 303.

48. Hopkins, "I Wake and Feel," ll. 6–8, 9–10, in *MW*, 166.

49. For a philosophical exploration of this concept, see Charles Taylor, *Sources of the Self: The Making of Modern Identity* (Cambridge, MA: Harvard University Press, 1989).

50. Hopkins, retreat notes, January 2, 1889, in *MW*, 303.

51. Hopkins, "I Wake and Feel," l. 12, in *MW*, 166.

52. Hopkins, "I Wake and Feel," ll. 13–14, in *MW*, 166.

53. Hopkins, "No Worst," ll. 1, 3, in *MW*, 167.

54. Hopkins, "No Worst," ll. 9–11, in *MW*, 167.

55. Hopkins, "No Worst," ll. 12–13, in *MW*, 167.

56. Hopkins to Bridges, February 17, 1887, in *MW*, 266–67.

57. Hopkins to Bridges, February 18, 1887, in *MW*, 268.

58. Hopkins, "(Carrion Comfort)," ll. 1–4, in *MW*, 168.

59. Hopkins, "Retreat at Beaumont," September 10, 1883, in *MW*, 301.

60. Hopkins, "On Death," in *MW*, 300.

61. Hopkins, "(Carrion Comfort)," ll. 5–8, in *MW*, 168.

62. The term is Hopkins's. See Hopkins to Dixon, December 22, 1880, *MW*, 243: "In lyric verse I like sprung rhythm also to be *over-rove*, that is the scanning to run on from line to line to the end of the stanza."

63. Hopkins, "(Carrion Comfort)," ll. 13–14, in *MW*, 168.

64. Frances Paravicini, quoted in *The Collected Works of Gerard Manley Hopkins*, 3:83.

65. Hopkins, "Justus quidem tu es, Domine," ll. 12–14, in *MW*, 183.

66. Written July 18, 1888.

67. Hopkins, "That Nature Is a Heraclitean Fire," ll. 9–11, in *MW*, 181.

68. Hopkins to Bridges, July 29–30, 1888, in *MW*, 386.

69. 2 Cor. 5:21. This theological construct is also called "the Great Exchange."

70. Hopkins, "That Nature Is a Heraclitean Fire," ll. 19–24, in *MW*, 181.

71. Hopkins, "As Kingfishers Catch Fire," ll. 9–14, in *MW*, 129; emphasis added.

Omega: Immortal Diamond

1. Hopkins, "To R.B.," l. 13, in *The Major Works, Including All the Poems and Selected Prose*, ed. Catherine Phillips (London: Oxford University Press, 2002), 184 (hereafter *MW*).

2. Robert Bernard Martin, *Gerard Manley Hopkins: A Very Private Life* (London: Faber & Faber, 2011), 415, quoting Hopkins's obituary.

3. His mother came to Ireland for the funeral, but only his father was permitted to attend, and the coffin was not allowed into the church due to the typhoid scare.

4. Many have speculated as to why the papers were burned the day after Hopkins's death. Homophobia has featured prominently as one reason. Robert Martin believes the Jesuits simply were unaware of the significance of the papers or of Hopkins's true talent. But today most scholars concur that this decision was taken to avoid possible infection or contamination from the illness.

5. Hopkins, "The Spiritual Exercises," August 7, 1882, in *MW*, 282.

Selected Bibliography

Ballinger, Philip A. *The Poem as Sacrament: The Theological Aesthetic of Gerard Manley Hopkins*. Louvain Theological and Pastoral Monographs 26. Louvain: Peeters; Grand Rapids: Eerdmans, 2000.

Balthasar, Hans Urs von. *The Glory of the Lord: A Theological Aesthetics*. Vol. 3, *Studies in Theological Style: Lay Styles*. San Francisco: Ignatius, 1986.

Barry, Michael. *Victorian Dublin Revealed: The Remarkable Legacy of Nineteenth-Century Dublin*. Dublin: Andalus, 2011.

Batchelor, John. *Tennyson: To Strive to Seek to Find*. New York: Pegasus Books, 2013.

Bate, Walter Jackson. *John Keats*. Oxford: Oxford University Press, 1966.

Bender, Todd. *Gerard Manley Hopkins: The Classical Background and Critical Reception of His Work*. Baltimore: Johns Hopkins University Press, 1966.

Bergonzi, Bernard. *Gerard Manley Hopkins*. New York: Macmillan, 1977.

Colley, Ann. *Victorians in the Mountains: Sinking the Sublime*. London: Ashgate, 2010.

Cook, Richard B. *The Grand Old Man*. Gloucestershire, UK: Dodo, 1898.

Downes, David A. *Gerard Manley Hopkins: A Study of His Ignatian Spirit*. New York: Bookman Associates, 1959.

DuBois, Martin. *Gerard Manley Hopkins and the Poetry of Religious Experience*. Cambridge: Cambridge University Press, 2017.

Easson, Angus. *Gerard Manley Hopkins*. Routledge Guides to Literature. London: Routledge, 2011.

Fiddes, Paul. "Gerard Manley Hopkins." In *The Blackwood Companion to the Bible in English Literature*, edited by Rebecca Lemon et al., 563–76. Chichester, UK: Wiley-Blackwell, 2009.

Fleming, Lenore Marie. "The Influence of Duns Scotus on Gerard Manley Hopkins." PhD diss., Loyola University, 1954.

Fordham, Finn. *I Do, I Undo, I Redo: The Textual Genesis of Modernism in Hopkins, Yeats, Conrad, Forster, Joyce, and Wolff*. New York: Oxford University Press, 2010.

Gardner, W. H. *Gerard Manley Hopkins: A Study in Poetic Idiosyncrasy in Relation to Poetic Tradition*. London: Oxford University Press, 1949.

Goodman, Ruth. *How to Be a Victorian: A Dawn-to-Dusk Guide to Victorian Life*. London: Norton, 2013.

Heuser, Alan. *The Shaping Vision of Gerard Manley Hopkins*. Oxford: Oxford University Press, 1958.

Hopkins, Gerard Manley. *The Collected Works of Gerard Manley Hopkins*. Edited by Leslie Higgins, Michael Suarez, SJ, Catherine Phillips, et al. Vols. 1–8. Oxford: Oxford University Press, 2006–2018.

———. *The Correspondence of Gerard Manley Hopkins and Richard Watson Dixon*. Edited by Claude Colleer Abbot. Oxford: Oxford University Press, 1935.

———. *The Early Poetic Manuscripts and Note-books of Gerard Manley Hopkins in Facsimile*. Edited by Norman MacKenzie. New York: Garland, 1989.

———. *Further Letters of Gerard Manley Hopkins Including His Correspondence with Coventry Patmore*. Edited by Claude Colleer Abbott. Oxford: Oxford University Press, 1956.

———. *The Journals and Papers of Gerard Manley Hopkins*. Edited by Sir Humphrey House. Oxford: Oxford University Press, 1959.

————. *The Later Poetic Manuscripts of Gerard Manley Hopkins in Facsimile.* Edited by Norman MacKenzie. New York: Garland, 1991.

————. *The Letters of Gerard Manley Hopkins to Robert Bridges.* Edited by Claude Colleer Abbot. Oxford: Oxford University Press, 1955.

————. *The Major Works, Including All the Poems and Selected Prose.* Edited by Catherine Phillips. London: Oxford University Press, 2002.

————. *Poems of Gerard Manley Hopkins.* Edited by W. H. Gardner and N. H. MacKenzie. Oxford: Oxford University Press, 1967.

Hughes, Glenn. *A More Beautiful Question: The Spiritual in Poetry and Art.* Columbia: University of Missouri Press, 2011.

Ignatius of Loyola. *The Letters of St. Ignatius of Loyola.* Edited and translated by William J. Young, SJ. Chicago: Loyola University Press, 1959.

————. *The Spiritual Exercises.* Edited by Elder Mullen. North Charleston, SC: First Rate Publishers, 2014.

Kitchen, Paddy. *Gerard Manley Hopkins.* London: Oxford University Press, 1978.

Kumiko, Tanabe. *Gerard Manley Hopkins and His Poetics of Fancy.* Cambridge: Cambridge University Press, 2015.

Lightman, Maria. *The Contemplative Poetry of Gerard Manley Hopkins.* Princeton: Princeton University Press, 1989.

Llewelyn, John. *Gerard Manley Hopkins and the Spell of John Duns Scotus.* Edinburgh: Edinburgh University Press, 2015.

Loomis, Jeffrey. *DaySpring in Darkness: Sacrament in Hopkins.* Lewisburg, PA: Bucknell University Press, 1988.

Mariani, Paul. *Gerard Manley Hopkins: A Life.* New York: Viking, 2008.

Martin, Robert Bernard. *Gerard Manley Hopkins: A Very Private Life.* New York: Putnam, 1991.

McDermott, John. *A Hopkins Chronology.* New York: St. Martin's, 1997.

Newman, John Henry. *An Essay in Aid of a Grammar of Assent.* Oxford: Oxford University Press, 1985.

Nisbet, Delia F. "Gerard Manley Hopkins and a Nun Named Gertrude." Hopkins Lectures, 2002. www.gerardmanleyhopkins .org/lectures/2002.

Pick, John. *Gerard Manley Hopkins: Priest and Poet*. Oxford: Oxford University Press, 1942.

Pomplun, Trent. "The Theology of Gerard Manley Hopkins: From John Duns Scotus to the Baroque." *Journal of Religion* 95, no. 1 (January 2015): 1–34.

Roe, Dinah. *The Pre-Raphaelites from Rossetti to Ruskin*. London: Penguin Books, 2010.

Ruskin, John. *Selected Writings*. Edited by Dinah Birch. Oxford: Oxford University Press, 2004.

Sagar, Keith. "Hopkins and the Religion of the Diamond Body." In *Literature and the Crime against Nature*. London: Chaucer, 2005.

Saville, Julia. *Queer Chevalier: The Homoerotic Asceticism of Gerard Manley Hopkins*. Charlottesville: University of Virginia Press, 2000.

Scotus, Duns. *Duns Scotus on Divine Love: Texts and Commentaries on Goodness and Freedom, God and Humans*. Edited by A. Vos and H. Veldhuis. London: Ashgate, 2003.

———. *God and Creatures: The Quodlibetal Questions*. Princeton: Princeton University Press, 1975.

Soboloev, Dennis. "Gerard Manley Hopkins and the Language of Mysticism." *Christianity and Literature* 53, no. 4 (Summer 2004): 455–86.

Thomas, Alfred, SJ. *Hopkins the Jesuit: The Years of Training*. Oxford: Oxford University Press, 1969.

Underhill, Evelyn. *The Essentials of Mysticism and Other Essays: The Mystic as Creative Artist*. London: Kessinger Legacy Reprints, 1920.

Weynand, Norman. *Immortal Diamond: Studies in Gerard Manley Hopkins*. London: Sheed & Ward, 1949.

Wilson, A. N. *The Victorians*. London: Norton, 2003.

Index

Titles published in the

LIBRARY OF RELIGIOUS BIOGRAPHY SERIES

Abraham Lincoln: Redeemer President
by Allen C. Guelzo

The First American Evangelical: A Short Life of Cotton Mather
by Rick Kennedy

Aimee Semple McPherson: Everybody's Sister
by Edith L. Blumhofer

Damning Words: The Life and Religious Times of H. L. Mencken
by D. G. Hart

Thomas Merton and the Monastic Vision
by Lawrence S. Cunningham

God's Strange Work: William Miller and the End of the World
by David L. Rowe

Blaise Pascal: Reasons of the Heart
by Marvin R. O'Connell

Occupy Until I Come: A. T. Pierson and the Evangelization of the World
by Dana L. Robert

The Kingdom Is Always but Coming: A Life of Walter Rauschenbusch
by Christopher H. Evans

A Christian and a Democrat: A Religious Life of Franklin D. Roosevelt
by John F. Woolverton with James D. Bratt

Francis Schaeffer and the Shaping of Evangelical America
by Barry Hankins

Harriet Beecher Stowe: A Spiritual Life
by Nancy Koester

Billy Sunday and the Redemption of Urban America
by Lyle W. Dorsett

Assist Me to Proclaim: The Life and Hymns of Charles Wesley
by John R. Tyson

Prophetess of Health: A Study of Ellen G. White
by Ronald L. Numbers

George Whitefield: Evangelist for God and Empire
by Peter Y. Choi

*The Divine Dramatist: George Whitefield and the Rise
of Modern Evangelicalism* by Harry S. Stout

Liberty of Conscience: Roger Williams in America
by Edwin S. Gaustad